SALTRAM

Devon

THE NATIONAL TRUST

Acknowledgements

This guide has been written by Ceri Johnson, Assistant Historic Buildings Representative for Devon, with picture entries by Alastair Laing. The National Trust is very grateful to the following for their help: Gertrude Antell, who was in service at Saltram in the 1930s, Priscilla Bannochie, the Dean of Carlisle, Tracey Earl of Coutts & Co., the 6th Earl of Morley, the late Brigadier the Hon. Robin Parker, Major Thomas St Aubyn, Rex Thomas, and the staff of Saltram and the Plymouth & West Devon Record Office.

Photographs: National Trust pp. 56, 65; NT/Mark J. Rattenbury p.23; NT/Chris Vile pp. 36 (above), 42 (below), 44 Saltram, The Morley Collection (The National Trust) p.39; National Trust Photographic Library/Colin Burt p. 51; NTPL/John Hammond pp. 17, 24, 25, 45, 46, 52, 53, 54, 55 (above and below); NTPL/Rob Matheson pp. 1, 5 (above), 7, 8, 10, 14, 30, 35, 42 (above), 43, 48, 59, 62, 63; NTPL/Rupert Truman pp. 4, 5 (below), 6, 41, 61; NTPL/Andreas von Einsiedel front cover, pp. 9, 12, 13, 15, 19, 20, 21, 27, 28, 29, 31, 33, 36 (below), 37, 47, 58, back cover; Sir John Soane's Museum, London p. 49.

First published in Great Britain in 1998 by the National Trust

© 1998 The National Trust

Registered charity no. 205846

ISBN 978 1 84359 174 0

Reprinted 2008, 2009; revised 2001, 2005

Designed by James Shurmer

Phototypeset in Monotype Bembo Series 270 by Printessential Ltd, Smallfield, Surrey (18926)

Printed by Hawthornes for National Trust (Enterprises) Ltd, Heelis, Kemble Drive, Swindon Wilts SN2 2NA on Cocoon Silk made from 100% recycled paper

(*Front cover*) The Saloon

(*Title-page*) An Adam door-handle in the Saloon

(*Back cover*) The mantelpiece in the Morning Room

Bibliography

ANON., 'Saltram, Devonshire', *Country Life*, 23, 30 January 1926, pp. 124–33, 160–70.

ANON., *The Ladies Field*, 20 October 1900.

BOLTON, Arthur T., *The Architecture of Robert and James Adam*, London, 1922.

CORNFORTH, John, 'Saltram, Devon', *Country Life*, 27 April, 4, 11 May 1967, pp. 998–1001, 1064–8, 1160–4; 'The Making of the Saltram Landscape', *Country Life*, 14 September 1967, pp. 594–7.

CROFT-MURRAY, Edward, *Decorative Painting in England 1537–1837*, ii, London, 1970.

DUFFIN, Anne, *Faction & Faith: Politics & Religion of the Cornish Gentry Before the Civil War*, University of Exeter Press, 1996.

FLETCHER, Ronald, *The Parkers of Saltram 1769–89*, London, 1970.

GILBERT, Christopher, *The Life and Work of Thomas Chippendale*, London, 1978.

GILL, Crispin, *Plymouth River: A History of the Laira and Cattewater*, Tiverton, 1997.

GORE, St John, 'A Patron of Portrait and Landscape: The Picture Collection at Saltram House, Devon', *Country Life*, 2 June 1966, pp. 1386–8.

GRAY, Dr Todd, *The Garden History of Devon: An Illustrated Guide to Sources*, University of Exeter Press, 1995, pp. 196–9.

HARRIS, Helen, *The Industrial Archaeology of Dartmoor*, Newton Abbot, 1972, pp. 86–8, 91–2, 170, 175.

LAING, Alastair, *In Trust for the Nation*, London, 1995, pp. 30–1, 197, 236.

LATHAM, Charles, *In English Homes*, London, 1904.

LEVESON GOWER, Sir George, and PALMER, Iris, eds., *Hary-o: The Letters of Lady Harriet Cavendish 1796–1809*, London, 1940.

LUMMIS, Trevor and MARSH, Jan, *The Woman's Domain*, London, 1990, pp. 63–90.

MALLET, J. V. G., 'Wedgwood's Early Vases: The Collection at Saltram House, Devon', *Country Life*, 9 June 1966, pp. 1480–2.

MORRIS, Christopher, ed., *The Illustrated Journeys of Celia Fiennes c.1682–c.1712*, Exeter, 1982.

NEATBY, Nigel, ed., *The Saltram Collection*, London, 1977.

STEVENS, J., ed., *Journals of the 3rd Earl of Morley 1879–1904* [unpublished].

STILLMAN, Damie, *Decorative Work of Robert Adam*, London, 1973.

THOMAS, Rex, *Archaeological Survey of Saltram*, 1992 [unpublished].

CONTENTS

SALTRAM

Saltram stands high above the River Laira in a rolling and wooded park that now provides a precious green space on the outskirts of Plymouth. The house, with its magnificent decoration and original contents, was largely created between the 1740s and 1820s by three generations of the Parker family. Each made its own distinctive contribution without obliterating what its predecessors had done.

building with symmetrical Palladian façades, although its Tudor core can still be glimpsed behind them. The Parkers' new interiors were more delicate, with Rococo ceiling plasterwork in the Entrance Hall, Morning Room and Velvet Drawing Room, and Chinese wallpapers in the upstairs bedrooms.

JOHN AND LADY CATHERINE PARKER

PALLADIAN AND ROCOCO

Soon after John Parker inherited Saltram in 1743, he began remodelling the house with the encouragement and the money of his wealthy wife, Lady Catherine Poulett. They clothed the rambling old

THERESA AND THE 1ST LORD BORINGDON

NEO-CLASSICAL

The second John Parker succeeded his father in 1768 and in 1784 was created Lord Boringdon (as we shall refer to him throughout, for the sake of clarity). In 1769 he married Theresa Robinson, who came from an artistically minded family that

Palladian: The west front

Neo-classical: Robert Adam's 1768 design for the chimneypiece wall of the Saloon

advised on the embellishment of the house. For the next six years, until her tragically early death, Saltram enjoyed a brief golden era. Both were painted by Sir Joshua Reynolds, who had grown up near Saltram and became a close friend. The ten portraits in the house by Devon's greatest artist are among the glories of the picture collection, which grew rapidly with his advice.

In 1768 Lord Boringdon turned to Robert Adam, the most fashionable architect and interior designer of the day, to create a suite of Neo-classical rooms along the east front which reaches a climax in the Saloon. Adam designed almost everything – from the huge plasterwork ceiling and matching carpet to the ornate door-handles – and Saltram now preserves one of the finest Adam interiors in Britain. Boringdon collected china (now mostly displayed in the Mirror Room), to decorate his new rooms, and commissioned Nathaniel Richmond to lay out the present open parkland.

THE 1ST EARL AND COUNTESS OF MORLEY

REGENCY

The third John Parker inherited in 1788, becoming the 1st Earl of Morley in 1815. In 1819–20 he employed the Regency architect John Foulston to add the Entrance Porch to the south front and make the present Library out of two smaller rooms. His second wife, Frances, maintained the family's artistic traditions, being a talented watercolourist and copier of Old Master paintings (on show in the Velvet Drawing Room and her Boudoir upstairs).

The 1st Earl devoted most of his energies to improving the estate with ambitious, but expensive, engineering and industrial projects, which left the family heavily in debt.

RETRENCHMENT AND REVIVAL

Money became so short that the 3rd Earl was forced to let the house from 1861 to 1884, and could afford to return only after selling several of Saltram's finest paintings. The family fortunes improved in 1926, when the 4th Earl inherited Dorchester House in London and the famous Gloucestershire arboretum at Westonbirt through his mother, Margaret Holford. Like Plymouth, Saltram suffered from enemy bombing during the Second World War, and in 1951 the house, its contents and 291 acres of the park were accepted in lieu of death-duties by H.M. Treasury, which transferred them to the National Trust in 1957.

Regency: the Doric porch and the coat of arms in the pediment were added by the 1st Earl of Morley

TOUR OF THE HOUSE

The Exterior

THE EAST FRONT

From the stables, visitors take the path to the house, passing the east front to the right before arriving at the main entrance. The east front was built during John and Lady Catherine Parker's modernisation of the old house in the mid-eighteenth century, and provides little hint as to the sumptuousness of the decoration inside. It comprises a three-storey central block stepped forward between two pedimented wings of the same height, and the whole, very plain façade is dominated by the great Venetian window of the Saloon. The wing to the left of the central block has false windows which create a symmetrical façade and provide extra wall space inside for hanging pictures. The only embellishment is the use of rusticated quoins.

This, and the other two show fronts, have always been rendered – a traditional technique often used when cut stone would have been impractical or too costly. The render was last renewed in the 1950s, when a cement-based material was used, reflecting the building practices of the time. This has the disadvantage of trapping moisture in the walls. A project is now under way to remove the existing render and replace it with a traditional lime-based material, which allows moisture to evaporate.

THE SOUTH FRONT

The south front is the principal façade of the mid-eighteenth-century house. The dominant feature is the pediment, containing the family's coat of arms, cast in artificial Coade stone in 1812, and incorporating the motto '*Fideli certa merces*', meaning 'Certain is the reward of the faithful'. The coronet was added in 1816, after the 2nd Lord Boringdon became the 1st Earl of Morley. On either side of the central block are three bow-fronted bays of the same height. The entrance porch was built to a design by John Foulston in 1820. Its Doric portico, and anthemion decoration over the doors and the window above, are in the Greek Revival style.

The south and east fronts

The Entrance Hall

The Interior

THE ENTRANCE HALL

CHIMNEYPIECE

The painted stone chimneypiece sets the tone for the room. The predominance of sculpture gives it an austere grandeur to compensate, perhaps, for its relatively modest proportions. The chimneypiece, by Thomas Carter the Elder (active *c.*1729–56), contains a central tablet depicting *Androcles and the Lion*. The marble bust above is an eighteenth-century copy of an Antique original described in the nineteenth-century inventories as the Emperor Nerva. The seventeenth-century plasterwork over-mantel, showing a king making a sacrifice, was brought up to date in the 1740s with a Rococo frame.

CEILING AND OVERDOORS

The ceiling decoration, which dates from the 1740s, has a large central figure of Mercury, god of good fortune, wealth and roads, to welcome visitors. The four overdoors represent the Elements: earth (*Triumph of Venus*), air (*Astronomy*), fire (*Vulcan's Forge*) and water (*A Dolphin*). The curvilinear over-mantel frame and ceiling plasterwork may be by Francesco Vassalli (active in England, 1724–*c.*1760).

PICTURES

LEFT OF ENTRANCE DOOR:

213 THOMAS HUDSON (1701–79)
Lady Catherine Parker, née Poulett (1706–58)
Inscribed as being the daughter and heiress of the 1st Earl Poulett who married John Parker in 1725 and whose money helped to pay for the rebuilding of

7

Saltram in the 1740s. However, the age of the sitter when this portrait was painted (*c.*1755–60) suggests that it may alternatively be of her son's first wife, Frances Hort (d.1764). She is painted in seventeenth-century 'Vandyke dress', inspired by Rubens's *Portrait of Hélène Fourment* (then thought to be by Van Dyck).

RIGHT OF ENTRANCE DOOR, AS YOU FACE IT:

205 Manner of THOMAS HUDSON (1701–79)
John Parker, later 1st Lord Boringdon (1734/5–88)
He commissioned Robert Adam to transform the interior of Saltram after he inherited the house in 1768.

SCULPTURE

CLOCKWISE FROM FIREPLACE:

Cicero; Apollo; Venus; John, 1st Earl of Morley (1772–1840) by Joseph Nollekens, signed and dated 1806.

Mercury, god of fortune, wealth and roads;
Rococo plasterwork on the Entrance Hall ceiling

FURNITURE

FLANKING ENTRANCE:

Pair of side-tables with serpentine tops of yellow marble and black painted frames, *c.*1750–75.

AGAINST LEFT- AND RIGHT-HAND WALLS:

Two Georgian mahogany marble-topped tables on cabriole legs.

Mahogany hall-chairs decorated with the 1st Earl's coat of arms.

CERAMICS

ON SIDE-TABLES:

Pair of Dutch Delft vases, late seventeenth-century.

Pair of Chinese vases Ming/Ching, *c.*1650.

OTHER

ON LEFT-HAND WALL:

Boulle bracket clock, *c.*1740, with movement by Etienne le Noir.

LEFT OF FIREPLACE:

Stick barometer by Thomas Jones (1775–1852).

THE MORNING ROOM

After the cool elegance of the Entrance Hall, the Morning Room provides a contrast in the richness and warmth of its decoration. The close-hanging of pictures on red velvet walls was fashionable at the time when this room was created in the 1740s. The chimneypiece, attributed to Sir Henry Cheere (1703–81), and plaster ceiling on the theme of music also date from this period.

In 1809 the future 1st Countess of Morley decided to modernise the room by covering the walls with a crimson flock wallpaper, and putting up the pier-glass and curtain poles. She thought the result 'a prodigious improvement', but by the end of the nineteenth century the family had had second thoughts, and the 3rd Earl of Morley put back the original Genoese silk velvet.

This was one of the rooms used for dining on occasions when the grandeur of the Dining Room was not required. In 1811 Lady Boringdon's brother, the Rev. Thomas Talbot, described a Morning Room dinner:

The Morning Room

His Ld.ship and Ly.ship seated opp. each other in the middle of the Table in the french taste: – in the Centre of the Table, *Nothing* – the first Course some white Soup opp. Ld. B. – some Soles opp. Ly. B. and nothing else – the 2nd [course] had small made dishes lengthwise of the table and nothing else – the 3rd [course] some Game and 3 or 4 small Dishes of sweet or savoury at Random – then the Dessert ... with some undrinkable Port, bad Madeira, Sherry and mediocre Claret planted at the 4 Corners – on a Side Table some Roast Mutton and boil'd Beef completed the Repast.

PICTURES

The collection was begun by the first John Parker, for whom Reynolds bought pictures when he was in Italy (1750–2). But the chief collector was undoubtedly his son, Lord Boringdon, no doubt originally on his Grand Tour in 1764, and then subsequently from, and with the advice of, Reynolds, and in the salerooms. He was also a patron of Reynolds and Angelica Kauffman, and the group of portraits by Reynolds constitutes one of the glories of Saltram.

Several of the star items were sold in the nineteenth century, and the National Trust was compelled by the Government to sell more, of lesser importance, in 1957 to raise an endowment. But an impression of how this major collection must have appeared in its heyday is still preserved in the ground-floor rooms and on the Staircase. About two-thirds of the pictures in the Morning Room are still in the same positions as they were in 1819.

(A detailed handlist of all the pictures on show is also available.)

ENTRANCE WALL:

4 GUIDO RENI (1575–1642)
? St Ursula
Possibly one of the unfinished paintings left in the artist's studio on his death and completed by a studio hand. By legend, St Ursula was a British princess martyred with 11,000 virgins at Cologne.

6 Sir JOSHUA REYNOLDS, PRA (1723–92)
The Hon. Theresa Parker (1744/5–75), and her son, John, later 1st Earl of Morley (1772–1840)
Theresa Parker was originally painted in 1772 on her own in a yellow dress: she thought she looked 'melancholy and sick'. In 1775 her son, then aged three, was added, and the dress repainted.

7 SASSOFERRATO (1609–85) after RAPHAEL (1483–1520)
Madonna and Child
A variant in reverse of the *Madonna della Sedia* (Pitti Palace, Florence), which was much venerated in the eighteenth and nineteenth centuries.

CHIMNEYPIECE WALL:

12 After GUERCINO (1591–1666)
Madonna and Child with the infant St John the Baptist
Once in the collection of Reynolds, who gave or sold it to his friend, Lord Boringdon. The original, painted in 1615/16, is in the National Gallery of Scotland, Edinburgh.

Sir JOSHUA REYNOLDS, PRA (1723–92)
13 *Montagu Edmund Parker (1737–1813)*, 1768
Lord Boringdon's younger brother, who lived at Whiteway, near Chudleigh. Painted in hunt uniform according to his sister-in-law, he 'seldom shines in conversation, but in woodcock season'.

OVER CHIMNEYPIECE:

18 *John Parker, later 1st Earl of Morley (1772–1840), and his sister Theresa (1775–1856) as Children*
The children of the 1st Lord Boringdon and his second wife. Painted in 1779, when John was seven and Theresa four. Their aunt said of it: 'They are very near kissing – an attitude they are very often in.'

21 *Francesco Bartolozzi, RA (1727–1815)*, 1771/2
A leading engraver, who reproduced many of Reynolds's portraits.

FAR WALL:

29 *John Parker, 1st Lord Boringdon (1734/5–88), c.1763–8*
Boringdon was a close friend of Reynolds, who very rarely painted portraits on such an intimate scale. In 1770 they went shooting together at Saltram, betting on who was the finer shot.

CERAMICS

ON CHIMNEYPIECE:

Pair of Wedgwood black basalt ware vases in the form of classical lamps supported by slaves, c.1780. The figures were based on those on a crucifix designed by the sixteenth-century goldsmith Antonio Gentile, but then thought to be by Michelangelo.

Pair of black basalt ware vases with pistol handles by Wedgwood's rival, Humphrey Palmer, c.1770.

METALWORK

ON CHIMNEYPIECE:

Bronze of Andromeda, Flemish or German, c.1600.

St Ursula by Guido Reni (Morning Room, 4)

FURNITURE

English lacquer cabinet on stand, c.1690.

Pair of gilded side-tables. The frames are English, the tops Florentine, inlaid with specimen marbles and mosaic pastoral scenes.

Mahogany dining-table, mid-eighteenth-century.

Four of a set of Gothick mahogany dining-chairs, c.1760.

Pair of mahogany cabinets in the Chippendale style, c.1760.

Four of a set of Chippendale-style dining-chairs, c.1760.

THE VELVET DRAWING ROOM

This was probably the principal drawing-room before the Saloon was added by Adam in 1768. The present decorative scheme closely resembles the appearance of the room in 1770, when Lord Boringdon's wife, Theresa, 'with her usual taste orderd all the mouldings, & parts of the Capitals of the Columns to be Gilt, which makes the Room much chearfuller & handsommer'. A portion of the original red silk velvet hangings (which were replaced by the present red flock in the 1950s) survives on the wall by the entrance to the Saloon. Adam designed the pair of gilt mirrors and tables beyond the columns to announce his grand new room – the tables were made by Joseph Perfetti in 1772.

The carpet and hearth-rug were bought in 1902 from Turbeville Smith of London.

CEILING

The mid-eighteenth-century ceiling is decorated with four putti carrying emblems of the Seasons.

CHIMNEYPIECE

The chimneypiece, attributed to Thomas Carter the Younger (d.1795), contains a late eighteenth-century basket grate and fender, which are mounted with paktong, a nickel-silver alloy which is not tarnished by the heat.

PICTURES

The walls have been crowded with pictures for many years, and included, in the time of the 1st Earl, many of his wife Frances' copies of Old Master paintings. Visitors expected to be informed about each picture, and in 1797 the 1st Earl's sister, Theresa Parker, described their new method:

We are about a great work here, which you would like to assist in very much ... viz: making Skreens! Tis an idea of *His Lordship's*, executed by us, and is meant to facilitate the explanation of the Pictures, the side of the room being represented on the Skreen, and the names of the pictures written inside the frames. The *architectural* parts, such as doors, chimneys, pilasters, etc., fall to my lot, the writing to Lady Elizabeth Moncke, and the pasting is a joint performance in which my Aunt has great share. We have been hard at work the whole morning.

WALL OPPOSITE CHIMNEYPIECE, LEFT OF DOOR, TOP:

56 EGBERT VAN HEEMSKERCK (c.1635–1704)
A Quaker Meeting, 1678
Heemskerck depicts himself holding palette and brushes in the bottom left-hand corner, and mocking an old woman having a religious fit.

RIGHT OF DOOR:

40 Manner of CANALETTO (1697–1768)
The Piazzetta seen from the Bacino, with the Booths of a Fair
A Venetian view typical of those produced by Canaletto and his rivals and imitators for Grand Tour visitors like Lord Boringdon.

57 Attributed to PIETER DE HOOCH (1629–84)
'The Empty Jug': Tavern Scene, with Serving-wench, Gentleman with Pipe and Dog, and Card Players
Such scenes have an implicit, moral message. The man's costume dates the picture to the 1670s, but it relates better to de Hooch's early works, which were inspired by the tavern and guardroom scenes of his Rotterdam senior, Ludolf de Jongh (1616–79), who may have even painted this picture.

WITHIN COLUMNS:

43 GABRIELE RICCIARDELLI (active 1741–77)
Views of Naples

ON LEFT, TOP TO BOTTOM:

(a) *The Chiaia from the West*

(b) *The Ponte Nuove in the Porto Grande*

The Velvet Drawing Room

ON RIGHT, TOP TO BOTTOM:

(c) *The Bay of Naples from the West, with the Abbey of San Martino and Castel Sant' Elmo in the Distance*

(d) *The Bay of Naples from the East, with Vesuvius in the Distance*

A set of engravings after paintings by Ricciardelli of the same views, but with different figures, was published in 1765.

CHIMNEYPIECE WALL:

401 C. A. RUTHART (*c.*1630–after 1703)
Lion attacking a Horse, 1672

49 Manner of CANALETTO (1697–1768)
Piazza del Popolo, Rome
Pendant to no. 41 opposite. Canaletto visited Rome in 1719–20 and possibly in 1742, but never painted this view of the piazza reorganised by Giuseppe

Valadier in 1816–20. The inverted conical chimney-tops betray the artist's Venetian origin.

FRANCES TALBOT, COUNTESS OF MORLEY (1782–1857) after DAVID TENIERS the Younger (1610–90)

50 *Peasant reading (The Sense of Sight)*

52 *A Gardener (The Sense of Smell)*
Two from a set of the *Five Senses.* The sole survivors here of Lady Morley's copies in oil of Old Masters.

51 ?
Miss Meyer as Hebe
Attributed to Angelica Kauffman in the 19th century, this painting is now thought to be possibly by Frances Talbot, after Sir Joshua Reynolds.

RIGHT OF CHIMNEYPIECE:

48 WILLEM II VAN NIEULANDT (1584–1635/6)
View of the Colosseum
The only painting by this interesting artist, poet and

dramatist in a British public collection. He was in Rome in 1602–5, working with Paul Bril, and subsequently lived off the images of the sites that he then recorded.

174 CHRISTOPH VAN DER LAMEN
(c.1606–1651/2)
A Tavern Scene: three men and a woman playing cards

FURNITURE

WALL OPPOSITE CHIMNEYPIECE TO
LEFT OF DOOR:
*Chippendale mahogany inlaid card-table, c.*1760.

TO RIGHT OF DOOR:
Giltwood side-table with scagliola top decorated with *trompe-l'oeil* cards, counters and a letter dated 2 May 1713 signed by John Pollexfen Junior, referring to the Treaty of Utrecht between France, England and Holland. The table may have come to Saltram through the Parkers' connection with nearby Kitley, then the home of the Pollexfens.
*Suite of gilded armchairs and window seats, c.*1775. The chairs retain their original red velvet.

IN MIDDLE OF BOW:
Late eighteenth-century mahogany Pembroke table, the top veneered in a feather pattern and inlaid with

A scagliola table-top decorated with trompe-l'oeil playing cards in the Velvet Drawing Room

lunettes and fan-shaped ornaments in ebony and boxwood.

RIGHT OF FIREPLACE:
Double-topped 'Harlequin' writing-table, possibly of cherrywood. The interior contains a secretaire fitment of small drawers and pigeon holes, which rises up on the movement of a catch. Made by Abraham Roentgen, c.1755.

LEFT OF FIREPLACE:
Boulle writing-desk, in the Louis XIV style.

ON BOULLE WRITING-DESK:
Watch in a Boulle case, late seventeenth-century, movement signed by Thomas Tompion (1639–1713), the most famous English clockmaker of the period.

CERAMICS AND SCULPTURE

ON HARLEQUIN TABLE:
Set of four Florentine bronze statuettes representing the Seasons, on Sienna marble bases.

ON MANTELSHELF:
Pair of famille verte Dogs of Fo, eighteenth-century.
Pair of white Chinese porcelain seated hounds, mid-eighteenth-century.
K'ang Hsi (1662–1722) blanc-de-Chine group of Kuan Yin the Maternal, with a boy on her lap.

ON GILT TABLES BEYOND THE COLUMNS:
Pair of early eighteenth-century French bronzes: *Amphitrite* after Michel Anguier; *Satyr* after a classical statue in the Louvre.

THE SALOON

The Saloon, or Great Drawing Room, was a formal room intended for entertaining, and would have been the high point of any visit to the house. The Countess of Morley described a ball held here in 1810, before the chandeliers were introduced:

The Saloon was prepared for the dancing and looked quite brilliant and beautiful – We lighted it by hanging lamps over the windows and putting a quantity of candles over the doors, the places in which they were fixed being concealed by large wreaths and festoons of leaves and flowers beautiful to behold. The floor was

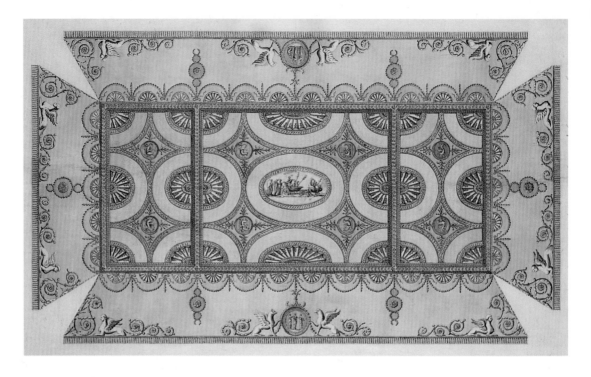

Adam's design for the Saloon ceiling

chalked after an exquisite design of my own, by a celebrated artist from Plymouth – out of the great window we had a temporary place erected for the North Devon Band which played the dances all night – round the room we had two rows of seats affording comfortable anchorage for about 200 persons.

This and the next room were Robert Adam's first commission at Saltram, and no expense was spared. His approach was to design as much as possible himself, ensuring the different elements came together as a coherent scheme. In 1768 he produced a full set of drawings for the wall elevations, ceilings and chimneypiece, which were modified to suit his client's taste.

CEILING

Lord Boringdon opted for a bold, simplified ceiling design, centred on three ovals, each containing a lozenge and a roundel. The roundel paintings are by Antonio Zucchi (1726–95), a regular collaborator with Adam and later Angelica Kauffman's husband (see p. 48). Acknowledging Lord Boringdon's love of hunting, the five paintings in the centre compart-

ment represent *Diana Hunting*, surrounded by *The Seasons*; in the other two lozenges are *Venus and Adonis* and the *Death of Procris*; in the cove, over the Venetian window and the fireplace, are the *Triumphs of Neptune* and of *Thetis*. The plaster-work here and in the Dining Room is attributed to Joseph Rose, who was paid £434 between 1770 and 1772.

CARPET

After the ceiling, Adam designed the carpet, made by Thomas Witty at Axminster for £126. It measures 46 feet by 22 feet, and its central lozenge and roundel were intended to echo the ceiling design. The movable furniture would have been arranged around the walls so that the carpet could be properly appreciated.

WALL-COVERINGS

The bright colours of the carpet were accentuated by the contrast with the pale blue damask on the walls, which was purchased in 1770 for £300. By 1811 it had faded to a 'rich dove' colour, and later in the nineteenth century a striped silk was put up, only to be replaced in 1950 by a new, pale blue damask.

The Venetian window in the Saloon

PIER-GLASSES

For the window wall, Adam designed four great pier-glasses – huge sheets of glass, eight feet in height, which would have been extravagantly expensive, and more costly than Lord Boringdon's initial choice of smaller, oval-shaped mirrors. Two of the pier-glasses were moved to the opposite wall, either side of the fireplace, probably in 1840, after the succession of the 2nd Earl.

DOORCASES AND WINDOW SURROUND

Adam was responsible for the doorcases and the Venetian window surround, all composed of double-guilloche pilasters, with capitals copied from Diocletian's palace at Split, and an anthemion frieze matching the room cornice. The fine gilded door-handles are based on a design illustrated in the second volume of Adam's *Works in Architecture* (1779).

CHIMNEYPIECE

Adam produced a design for a matching chimney-piece, but it was never executed, since the present chimneypiece, attributed to Thomas Carter the Younger, was already in place. The columns and frieze are of red brescia marble, and the central relief depicts the *Choice of Hercules*. The Neo-classical basket grate, fender and fire-irons are all mounted with paktong.

LIGHTING

During the nineteenth century, the chandeliers were introduced, and the Venetian window was turned into a door, with a stained-glass lunette. In the 1960s the Trust removed the stained glass and reglazed the window in its original proportions.

PICTURES

Adam seems to have initially envisaged only inset overmantel and overdoor paintings, but the Parkers decided to hang Old Masters and Old Master copies here, combined with the most prestigious portraits from the present and past.

FAR WALL, LEFT OF DOOR, ABOVE:

76 Sir JOSHUA REYNOLDS, PRA (1723–92)
The Hon. Theresa Parker (1744/5–75)
Painted between April 1770 and March 1772, to hang in the Saloon as the pendant of the *Sir Thomas Parker*, as it still does. There was a terrible premonition of her early death in the pose, of which she wrote to her brother: 'Mr. Parker says I am drawn feeling my pulse: it may not be the less like for that, as I am apt to do so.' In an obituary, Reynolds wrote: 'Her amiable disposition, her softness and gentleness of manners, endeared her to every one that had the happiness of knowing her.'

FLANKING DOOR, BELOW:

Attributed to NICCOLÒ CODAZZI (1642–93) and another hand

LEFT: 91 *Classical Ruins with Beggars and a Fortune-teller*

RIGHT: 77 *Architectural Capriccio with the Arch of Titus*

Codazzi's father Viviano (*c*.1604–70) invented these kinds of paintings of usually ruined architecture, with figures painted by another artist.

OVER DOOR:

92 After TITIAN (1488/90–1576)
Danäe
Danäe was the daughter of Acrisius, King of Argos, who had been told by an oracle that any son she bore would kill him. He locked her in a tower with only slits for windows, through which Zeus is shown impregnating her in the form of a golden shower. Perseus, the son born of this union, inadvertently killed his grandfather with a discus. The original picture is in the Museo di Capodimonte in Naples.

RIGHT OF DOOR, ABOVE:

90 MARCUS GHEERAERTS the Younger (1561/2–1635/6)
Sir Thomas Parker
Inscribed 'Sir Thomas Parker b:1595' and traditionally thought to be the second son of John Parker of North Molton. But he was never knighted and was born in 1593/4, and so it is more probably of the unrelated Sir Thomas Parker of Ratton in Sussex (b.1594/5).

CHIMNEYPIECE WALL, OVER LEFT-HAND DOOR:

78 Sir JOSHUA REYNOLDS, PRA (1723–92) and studio
Sir Thomas Acland, 7th Bt (1723–85), 1768(?)
A neighbouring landowner and friend of the Parkers.

The magnificent frame to the early copy of Titian's The Andrians *was probably designed by Adam and made by Chippendale (79)*

OVER CHIMNEYPIECE:

79 After TITIAN (1488/90–1576)
The Andrians
The Andrians inhabited the Aegean island of Andros, famous for its wine in Antiquity. Titian shows them celebrating the annual visit of Dionysus, god of wine (his ship can be seen in the distance), when a fountain of water turned into wine. A good early copy of the picture now in the Prado in Madrid, said to have been acquired from Reynolds. The superb frame was probably designed by Adam and carved by Chippendale.

OVER RIGHT-HAND DOOR:

80 Sir JOSHUA REYNOLDS, PRA (1723–92) and studio
William, 2nd Earl of Shelburne, later 1st Marquess of Lansdowne (1737–1805)
An Oxford contemporary and close friend of Lord Boringdon, he was Prime Minister in 1782–3, but remained a solitary and mistrusted political figure.

NEAR WALL, LEFT OF DOOR:

81 Studio of Sir PETER PAUL RUBENS (1577–1640) and FRANS SNYDERS (1579–1657)
Three Huntresses returning from the Chase
Probably painted around 1617 by Snyders himself, with the collaboration of Rubens's studio for the figures, under the master's own supervision.

82 Manner of PIETER NEEFFS the Elder (active 1605–56/61)
Interior of Antwerp Cathedral
Neeffs and his son, also Pieter (1620–after 1675), both painted innumerable cathedral interiors more or less loosely based on that of Antwerp before the introduction of Rubens's great altarpieces.

OVER DOOR TO VELVET DRAWING ROOM:

83 ADAM FRANS VAN DER MEULEN (1632–90)
The Siege of Maastricht
The artist may have witnessed the taking of the Dutch city by Louis XIV's army in 1673.

RIGHT OF DOOR TO VELVET DRAWING ROOM,
ABOVE:

84 After RAPHAEL (1483–1520)
St John in the Wilderness
A late copy of the picture in the Uffizi in Florence.

BELOW:

85 Attributed to BARTOLOMEO PASSEROTTI
(1529–92)
A Group of Six Men
Probably not a family, but a group of *virtuosi*. The
third man from the left may be a self-portrait.

WINDOW WALL:

87 Sir JOSHUA REYNOLDS, PRA (1723–92)
Admiral Paul Ourry, MP (1719–83)
The father of Charity, who married Montagu
Edmund Parker, younger brother of Lord Boring-
don. Painted early in Reynolds's career, probably
*c.*1748.

FURNITURE

Giltwood suite of eighteen armchairs and two sofas,
attributed to Thomas Chippendale (*c.*1718–79).
Five payments to Chippendale, amounting to £225,
are recorded in Lord Boringdon's account books
for 1771 and 1772.

Pair of giltwood side-tables, probably based on a
design by Adam, with frames made by Joseph
Perfetti (he received £41 1s in 1771 'for Table
Frames for the Great Room'). The tops are Florentine and inlaid with coloured marbles.

Set of four six-branch candelabra, made by Matthew
Boulton (1728–1809) in 1772 as a version of the
design for George III of a pair of candelabra (known
as the 'King's vases'), now at Windsor Castle. The
bodies are bluejohn (Derbyshire felspar) mounted
in ormolu. The gilded torchères, on which the
candelabra stand, are probably based on a design by
Adam.

SCULPTURE

ON MANTELPIECE:

Seven bronzes by Giacomo (*c.*1731–85) *and Giovanni
Zoffoli* (*c.*1745–1805), probably acquired by the 1st
Earl when he visited Italy *c.*1818. From left to right:
*The Borghese Vase, The Seated Agrippina, The Capi-
toline Flora, Marcus Aurelius on horseback, The
Farnese Flora, The Seated Menander* (then called
Sulla) and *The Medici Vase.*

CERAMICS

ON AND BENEATH SIDE-TABLES:

Nine pieces of Japanese Imari porcelain, five with lids
with figures. Late seventeenth-century.

*Since the Axminster carpet is now too fragile to be
walked on, visitors leave the Saloon by the door in the
south-west corner, and reach the Dining Room via the
East Corridor.*

THE EAST CORRIDOR

PICTURES

At the Staircase Hall end of the East Corridor is a set
of eight grisaille paintings of classical statuary by
Louis Gabriel Blanchet (1705–72). Further along
are some of Adam's drawings for the Saloon, the
design for a great house dedicated to Lady Catherine Parker, a drawing for an inkstand made for
Theresa Parker's brother, Thomas 2nd Lord
Grantham, in 1777 and a set of ten gouache early
19th-century classical figures.

THE DINING ROOM

When the family entertained important guests,
they used this formal Dining Room. One such
occasion, in 1811, was described by the Rev. Talbot:

… the table of an immense width with a plateau full of
biscuit figures & vases with flowers &c. the whole
length, leaving merely room for a dish at each end of a
single row of dishes round with 4 Ice vases with
Champagne &c. at the corners of it – the Cookery
very *recherchée*, blamange made of peach juice – & jelly
filled with little half dissolved flakes of pine, the rest in
the same high *goût*.

This room was designed by Adam in 1768–70 as
the Library, and only became the Dining Room ten
years later, when Lord Boringdon decided to bring
the eating-room within range of his new kitchen.
Judging by its design, Adam's involvement in the
new Dining Room was limited: he would not have
left such large spaces below the relief medallions,
nor would he have blocked two of the three windows in the bow. From the Library scheme, his
chimneypiece (probably executed by Thomas
Carter the Younger) and ceiling survived.

The Dining Room

The ceiling was designed by Adam, with plasterwork by Joseph Rose and lunette paintings by Antonio Zucchi

CEILING AND OVERDOORS

The four lunettes in the ceiling are painted with library-oriented classical subjects by Antonio Zucchi; reading clockwise they are: *Anacreon sacrificing to the Graces, Alexander instructing Aristotle to write the History of the Creation, Plato with his Pupils* and *Virgil reading the Aeneid to the Emperor Augustus and the fainting Octavia*. The medallion heads in the corners are the classical thinkers Socrates, Zeno, Cicero and Thales of Miletus. Zucchi also painted the overdoors, which depict, clockwise from over the door to the Saloon: *Diogenes casting away his Bowl, Aristippus and his shipwrecked Companions discovering geometrical Drawings in the Sand*, and *Metellus ordering a marble Crow to be placed on the Tomb of his Master, Diodorus, for teaching him to chatter instead of reason*. When the Library bookcases were removed to create the new Dining Room, Zucchi also supplied the six landscape and ruin cap-riccios to fill the spaces and accord with Zuccarelli's already-existing landscape overmantel.

By 1811 the Dining Room was 'painted in the Etruscan style', but is now in the earlier pale green.

VASES

For the new Dining Room, Adam designed the pair of green vases and pedestals which flank the sideboard in the bow and were used as wine-coolers.

CARPET

The carpet, by Thomas Whitty of Axminster, was probably made from a drawing of the finished ceiling, which it resembles closely in colour and design.

FURNITURE

Set of oval-backed mahogany chairs with leather seats, *c.*1780–5. When not in use, the chairs and table would have been removed or arranged around the walls.

Georgian mahogany dining-table on square, chamfered legs.

CERAMICS AND GLASS

ON MANTELPIECE:

Three 'pebble' vases, imitating natural stone, by Wedgwood & Bentley, *c.*1770–5.

ON DINING-TABLE, SIDEBOARD AND SIDE-TABLE:

Marseilles faience dinner service, painted in green with flowers and the Parker crest. Probably made at the Veuve Perrin factory, *c.*1750–70.

ON DINING-TABLE:

Pieces of late eighteenth-century English cut-glass, including star- and leaf-shaped pickle dishes.

SILVER

ON DINING-TABLE:

Set of George III candlesticks of Corinthian column form, engraved with the Parker crest, 1763.

OTHER

IN BOW NICHES:

Pair of Etruscan plaster urns, purchased from Peter Vannini in 1770 for £50.

Leave the Dining Room, descend the stairs, turn right into the Kitchen Court and then left into

THE GREAT KITCHEN

Since the eighteenth century, the north end of the house at ground level has contained the service areas. A house of Saltram's size required more than ten staff to run it.

In 1778 a fire at the north end of the house gave

The Great Kitchen

Lord Boringdon the opportunity to rationalise the domestic offices. The laundry and brew-house had been destroyed in the blaze, and in their place Lord Boringdon built a spacious new kitchen. Separated from the main house by its own hipped roof, the new kitchen was designed to minimise the risk of fire spreading, and to contain cooking smells. A new laundry and brew-house were built as a separate block further north. In 1811 the 1st Countess's brother described the result as 'immense & in the utmost order of neatness, the Kitchen with all its Appendent offices is a most complete thing'. The Kitchen was remodelled in 1913, and continued in use until the death of the 5th Earl in 1962.

The most striking feature is the *batterie de cuisine*, which comprises around 600 copper pans, moulds and utensils, many of which are marked 'B' for Boringdon. A large number of other kitchen utensils are displayed, reflecting the scale and variety of cuisine required for a grand country house. The great hearth incorporates an open range of about 1810, complete with roasting spits driven by heat from the fire and a large dripping pan to catch the fat. The cast-iron closed range in the middle of the room was made by Flavel & Co. of Leamington, and installed in 1885.

THE SCULLERY

This is fitted with two late nineteenth-century sinks, one of porcelain, the other lined with copper, for washing dishes.

THE BUTCHERY

This is furnished with a rack for hanging carcases on, a pallet for carrying them, and chopping tables.

Retrace your steps to the North Stairs

THE NORTH STAIRS

On these secondary stairs hang a variety of family portraits. A full list is available.

SECOND LANDING

208 GEORGE CHARLES MORLAND (1763–1804)
The Pretty Ballad Singer

THE DOLL'S HOUSE ROOM

The doll's house is believed to have been made for Emily Katherine Parker, daughter of the 2nd Earl of Morley in about 1850. It is traditionally associated with Whiteway, near Chudleigh, a house built in about 1770 for John Parker, later Lord Boringdon. The doll's house remained at Saltram until the time of the 5th Earl. It was eventually purchased by Vivien Greene, who gave it to the National Trust in 1998.

Proceed through the Children's Education Room and the Children's Activities Room to the Little Gallery, which is lined with a selection of work by contemporary artists. Details of this may be found in the room.

Visitors ascend the Red Stairs to the Lobby. On the wall is a portrait of Frances Talbot, Dowager Countess of Morley, surrounded by some of her watercolours.

THE BRIGADIER'S SITTING ROOM

This is one of the rooms previously occupied by Brigadier the Hon. Robin Michael Parker, the late brother of the present Earl. Still used as a sitting room, you are invited to pause here and browse through family albums and assorted literature in the room.

PICTURES

CHIMNEYPIECE WALL:

THOMAS PHILIPS, RA (1770–1845) after Opie
147 *Frances Talbot, later Countess of Morley, as Lavinia*
The portrait by Opie was exhibited at the Royal Academy in 1802.

The Whiteway Doll's House, c.1850 (Doll's House Room)

210 *John Parker, 1st Earl of Morley* (1772–1840)

WEST AND EAST WALLS:

WILLIAM TOMKINS, ARA (*c.*1732–92)
181 and 182 *Two Views of Whiteway*

WINDOW WALL, OPPOSITE CHIMNEYPIECE:

218 BENJAMIN BURNELL (1769–1828)
Henry, Son of the 1st Earl of Morley (1806–17)

THE STUDY

The Chinese wallpaper in this room dates from the eighteenth century and consists of a very rare arrangement of panels framed with key-patterned strips. It was used as a study by the 3rd Earl of Morley for his Parliamentary duties.

FURNITURE

AROUND WALLS:

*Six 'Chinese' Chippendale elbow chairs, c.*1760.

A late 18th-century mahogany secretaire bookcase, containing the 3rd Earl's parliamentary papers.

CERAMICS

ON TABLE:

Chinese famille rose punch bowl. Reign of Qianlong (1736–95).

CENTRE OF MANTELPIECE:

A blanc-de-chine porcelain figure of the Goddess Kuan Yin the Maternal. From the Tê-Hua factories, early eighteenth-century.

Return through the Brigadier's Sitting Room to the Green Dressing Room

Detail of an eighteenth-century Chinese wallpaper panel with a key-pattern border (The Study)

THE GREEN DRESSING ROOM

On enquiring at breakfast into the Cause of the most unbounded Peals of Laughter proceeding from all the Ladies assembled in her Dressing Room after their Retirement for the Night, we found it was excited by her imitation of *Dickey Drake*, the Hot Lobster Story ... etc.

The Rev. Talbot, 1811

In the nineteenth century, this was Lady Morley's Dressing Room. Hot water was brought up from the Scullery in the cans to fill the hip bath. The room now takes its name from the green wallpaper. It retains its Victorian gas lamps.

PICTURES

The walls are hung with engravings, many of portraits by Reynolds, which include two of those sold to boost Saltram's finances in the second half of the nineteenth century – *Mrs Abington* and *Kitty Fisher*.

LORD MORLEY'S ROOM

For many years, this room was called the Damask Room and was probably another living-room. Now that the damask has gone, the Trust has furnished it as a bedroom and renamed it Lord Morley's Room, after the 1st Earl, whose bedroom was elsewhere on the south front of the house. The chimneypiece and joinery are mid-eighteenth-century. The present wallpaper is a copy of the late nineteenth-century paper found here when the room was being restored.

PICTURES

NORTH WALL:

JOHN DOWNMAN, ARA (1750–1824)
John Parker, 2nd Lord Boringdon, later 1st Earl of Morley (1772–1840), 1805
In the uniform of the Devon Militia. In 1805 there were fears of French invasion, until dispelled by the Battle of Trafalgar.

DANIEL GARDNER (1750–1805)
John Parker, later 1st Earl of Morley (1772–1840), *as a Boy*, 1779

On 26 March 1779 Anne Robinson wrote to her brother: 'The Boy is sitting to Mr. Gardner in his regimentals, with an espontoon [pike], gorget [throat armour], and sash, like a little officer on guard.'

JOHN DOWNMAN, ARA (1750–1824)
Montagu Parker (1737–1813), 1780
Younger brother of Lord Boringdon.

Charity Ourry, Mrs Montagu Parker (1752–86), 1780
Daughter of Admiral Paul Ourry and wife of Montagu Parker, whom she married in 1775.

John Parker, later 1st Lord Boringdon (1734/5–88), 1780

? Henrietta Parker (d.1808), 1780
Probably Lord Boringdon's unmarried sister.

ALEXANDER BLAIKLEY (1816–1903)
Lady Katherine Parker (1846–1910)
Only daughter of the 2nd Earl.

Albert, Lord Boringdon, later 3rd Earl of Morley (1843–1905)
Succeeded as 3rd Earl in 1864.

The Hon. Anne Robinson, sister of the 1st Baron Boringdon's 2nd wife, Theresa (Lord Morley's Room)

Frances (Talbot), Dowager Countess of Morley
(1782–1857)
A skilled artist she continued to live at Saltram, painting watercolour copies, after the death of her husband, the 1st Earl.

RICHARD BUCKNER (1812–83)
Harriet (Parker), Countess of Morley (1809–97)
Married the 2nd Earl in 1842, and honeymooned in Rome, where this portrait was painted in 1843.

JOHN DOWNMAN, ARA (1750–1824)
? *Admiral Paul Ourry* (1719–93)
See no. 73, p. 18.

HUGH DOUGLAS HAMILTON (1736–1808)
The Hon. Theresa Parker (1744/5–75), 1771
Lord Boringdon's second wife, drawn two years after their marriage.

? After JOHN DOWNMAN, ARA (1750–1824)
The Hon. Anne Robinson (1742–after 1812)
After the death of her much-loved younger sister, Theresa, in 1775, Anne brought up the latter's children and ran the Saltram household.

FURNITURE

Late eighteenth-century mahogany four-poster bed, with modern chintz hangings. The posts are carved in the Chippendale style.

Mahogany serpentine-fronted night-table, c.1760.

RIGHT OF FIREPLACE:

Mahogany serpentine-fronted commode, the top drawer containing dressing-table fittings and an adjustable mirror. All the drawers have gilt brass handles and keyhole escutcheons of Chippendale chinoiserie design.

Mahogany inlaid break-front wardrobe, late eighteenth-century, with a later dentil cornice.

ON WINDOW WALL:

Secrétaire à abattant (writing cabinet) by the German *ébéniste* Maurice-Bernard Evalde, c.1770–4.

RIGHT OF COMMODE:

A Sheraton-style satinwood cabinet on four slender legs inlaid with marquetry ribbons, quivers and floral patterns in coloured woods. English, 1770–1810.

THE BOUDOIR

In the early nineteenth century, this room and others on the south front were used by the family as informal dining- and sitting-rooms. The Countess's brother described an afternoon here in 1811:

No domestic attends, some three footmen, a Maître d'Hotel and Valet de Chambre standing or *laying* on the great Gallery of the stair Case outside the Door, till summoned by a hem or whistle his Ld.ship performing by a Dumb Waiter the whole Ceremony himself – we remain in the Room while this host of Varlets remove the table and its contents ... & substitute a smaller one on which tea comes in an hour.

The Boudoir has been redecorated by the Trust to appear as it might have done in the 1860s. In the house inventory from that time, it is called Lady Morley's Sitting Room, after Frances, the 1st Countess, who spent her last years here.

PICTURES

Amongst her many accomplishments, the 1st Countess was a talented artist with a particular skill as a copyist, and is said to have studied with François Gérard in Paris. Many of her watercolours are on display here. They are chiefly views of picturesque sites on the Continent, after such artists as William Callow, T.S.Boys, Samuel Prout and David Roberts, and genre scenes in the manner of W.H.Hunt and Joshua Cristall. In 1809 she wrote to her sister-in-law, Theresa Villiers, with advice on drawing lessons for the Villiers children, to 'get a set of heads taken from Raphael's cartoons ... they are the very finest and best things they could copy ... let them draw them over and over again'.

FURNITURE

NEAR MIDDLE OF ROOM:

Early nineteenth-century rosewood loo (card) table draped with cream Chinese silk shawl, and displaying family photographs.

Rosewood work-table, the top laid with lacemaking and needlework tools, early nineteenth-century.

ON LEFT WALL:

Regency rosewood table with gilt bronze mounts and an inlaid marble top.

Mid-18th-century mahogany tallboy. The eleventh drawer from the base opens as a secretaire.

The Boudoir

CERAMICS AND GLASS

The Boudoir contains an interesting collection of Bow, Derby, Plymouth and Meissen figures. A full list is available in the room.

ON MANTELSHELF:

Two glass goblets, German or Russian, each engraved with a portrait of Empress Elizabeth Petrovna I of Russia (1741–61), mid-eighteenth-century.

THE CHINESE CHIPPENDALE BEDROOM

From the late eighteenth century, this room was called the Blue Bow, and has been used at different times as a bedroom and an informal sitting- or dining-room.

WALLPAPER

In the eighteenth century Chinese goods were imported by the East India Company, leading to confusion between Indian and Chinese objects, which were often displayed side by side, and inaccurately described – Chinese wallpaper was often called 'India paper'.

The wallpaper is a 'factory' paper – a type which represented scenes from daily life in China, particu-

The Chinese Chippendale Bedroom

larly industrial and agricultural activities. It is in fact silk, painted with figures hard at work growing, curing and packing tea. Chinese wallpapers which depicted people, rather than only birds and flowers, were the most expensive, and there are two at Saltram.

CHIMNEYPIECE

The mid-eighteenth-century chimneypiece is carved with the 'bears and bees' illustration of the proverb: 'Take what you want, says God. Take it, and pay for it.'

FURNITURE

Mahogany four-poster bed, c.1760, possibly supplied by Thomas Chippendale, with earlier needlework hangings.

Four chairs in the 'Chinese Chippendale' style, with pagoda-shaped cresting rails. Two are of padouk-wood.

'Chinese Chippendale' mahogany hanging shelves, designed for the display of porcelain.

Two George I mahogany chests-of-drawers.

PICTURES

AROUND CHIMNEYPIECE:

A group of mid-eighteenth-century Chinese mirror paintings, with contemporary English giltwood frames carved in Rococo style.

CERAMICS

ON MANTELPIECE:

K'ang Hsi blanc-de-Chine group of Kuan Yin the Maternal, with a boy on her lap.

ON EITHER SIDE:

Pair of Chinese porcelain figures of Immortals, eighteenth-century.

Pair of blanc-de-Chine figures of Dogs of Fo, seated with paws resting on brocade balls, early eighteenth-century.

THE CHINESE DRESSING ROOM

The partition dividing the room is an original feature, allowing easy access to the adjoining bedroom.

WALLPAPER

The wallpaper in the Chinese Dressing Room is thought to date from the beginning of the eighteenth century, and is probably the oldest in the house. The pattern is the 'Long Elizas' type, from the Dutch '*lange Lyzen*' ('tall women'), and is composed of unusually tall, elongated figures painted on mulberry paper. Close examination reveals that at some point the wallpaper has been added to, with birds and other shapes cut out of a different wallpaper and pasted over gaps in the design.

FURNITURE

RIGHT OF WINDOW:

Enclosed and fitted mahogany wash-stand, the top containing fittings for basins and glasses, and an adjustable toilet mirror.

NEAR MIDDLE OF ROOM:

Early nineteenth-century mahogany wash-stand, incorporating a wooden soap vase and cover over two small, triangular drawers.

OPPOSITE FIREPLACE:

Eighteenth-century mahogany dwarf wardrobe.

ON WARDROBE:

Early nineteenth-century mahogany portable medicine cabinet.

RIGHT OF FIREPLACE:

Chinese Chippendale padoukwood single chair, cut down in height, probably for use as a nursing chair.

CERAMICS

ON MANTELPIECE:

*Pair of Imari figures of Japanese women, c.*1700.

ON TOP OF MAHOGANY CHEST TO LEFT OF WINDOW:

Chinese porcelain famille rose jug, painted with an emperor and his court. Reign of Qianlong (1736–95).

The nineteenth-century medicine chest in the Chinese Dressing Room

IN ENCLOSED AND FITTED WASH-STAND:

Chinese porcelain famille rose jug of 'Monk's Cap' design (a shape derived from ritual vessels of the Ming period), eighteenth-century.

THE STAIRCASE HALL

The Staircase Hall was built for John Parker in the 1740s. Whoever the architect was, he seems to have had difficulty fitting the required classical elements into the available space. As a result, the pediments of the doorcases are crammed together, and the entablature of the great Doric columns juts out beyond the landing. The Rococo plasterwork ceiling is also mid-eighteenth-century, with the exception of the moulding around the skylight which is later. The skylight's iron frame was renewed in the late eighteenth century. The staircase balusters, handrail and panelling are mahogany, while the treads are deal.

During the time of Lord Boringdon, the Staircase Hall opened into the Velvet Drawing Room and Morning Room, as well as the Saloon and Entrance Hall. It was sufficiently grand to escape major alteration by Adam, although the mahogany joinery on the stairs seems to have been updated at this time. Theresa's brother, the 2nd Lord Grantham, was clearly impressed, and wrote to say: 'If ever Mr. Munro should go to England, I would advise him to go to Saltram, he is mahogony [sic] mad, the Doors, Staircase, & terms would turn his head.' By 1811, the Rev. Talbot thought the Staircase Hall and the Saloon 'equal to any thing one can see in the first Houses in England'. Today, the Staircase Hall is a showcase for some of the finest pictures in the Saltram collection.

PICTURES

TOP LANDING, RIGHT:

113 Sir PETER PAUL RUBENS (1577–1640)
Vincenzo II Gonzaga, Duke of Mantua (1594–1627)
The youngest son of Vincenzo I, he became a cardinal, but had to renounce this after it emerged that he had married a widow much older than himself. Succeeded to the dukedom in 1626, as the last of the line, and sold this picture and the rest of the great Mantuan collections to King Charles I, whose brand appears on the back of the panel.

Vincenzo II Gonzaga, Duke of Mantua; by Peter Paul Rubens (no. 113; Staircase Hall)

LEFT:

198 ANGELICA KAUFFMAN, RA (1741–1807)
Edmund Bastard of Kitley (1758–1816)
Neighbour and friend

TOP FLIGHT, ON LEFT:

111 JAKOB PHILIPP HACKERT (1737–1807)
View of the Plain of Caserta seen from the Royal Belvedere, 1785
The new palace of Caserta was built fifteen miles north of Naples from 1751 for Charles III and his successor Ferdinand IV of the Kingdom of the Two Sicilies.

OVER LANDING:

110 ANGELICA KAUFFMAN, RA (1741–1807)
Vortigern, King of Britain, enamoured of Rowena at the Banquet of Hengist, exh. 1770
So smitten was Vortigern with the Saxon King Hengist's daughter Rowena that he betrayed his own men to the invaders. Pendant to no. 106 and a similarly fanciful depiction of early English history.

SECOND FLIGHT OF STAIRS, ABOVE LEFT:

106 *Interview of Edgar and Elfrida after her Marriage to Athelwold*, exh. 1771
This fanciful, but pioneering, depiction of an episode from early English history helped to make Kauffman's reputation.

BELOW LEFT:

107 *Sir Joshua Reynolds*, PRA (1723–92), 1767
Painted in seventeenth-century dress with a bust of Michelangelo (the artist Reynolds revered above all others) and volumes of Johnson's *Idler*, Burke's *Sublime and the Beautiful* and Goldsmith's *Traveller* (Reynolds was a friend of all three authors). Reynolds is presented as the sociable figure so at ease in fashionable and literary circles. Probably commissioned by Lord Boringdon.

CENTRE TOP:

108 ORAZIO SAMACCHINI (c.1532–77)
Madonna and Child in Glory with St Petronius and Mary Magdalen
Originally the altarpiece of the Capella Maggiore in the church of S. Maria della Morte, Bologna. Brought to England in 1819 by the 1st Earl of Morley. St Petronius was one of the patron saints of Bologna.

The Staircase Hall

FIRST FLIGHT, LOWER REGISTER:

102 GEORGE STUBBS, ARA (1724–1806)
The Fall of Phaethon, 1777
Phaethon begged his father Apollo to be allowed to drive the chariot of the sun. He lost control, and to avoid disaster to the earth, Jupiter struck him in mid-career with a thunderbolt. A rare mythological subject by the great animal painter.

CENTRAL REGISTER, LEFT:

ANGELICA KAUFFMAN, RA (1741–1807)

101 *Ulysses discovering Achilles*, exh. 1769
Achilles had been disguised as a girl among the daughters of Lycomedes to avoid serving in the Trojan War (where he was fated to die), but betrayed his true sex by instinctively choosing the armour offered by Ulysses, rather than jewellery.

104 *Hector taking leave of Andromache*, exh. 1768
One of the climactic and most pathos-charged episodes in Homer's *Iliad*. Taking leave of his wife, Hector terrifies their young son Astyanax by donning his helmet, prior to his death at the hands of Achilles. Pendant to no. 101.

TOP REGISTER:

100 *Penelope taking down the Bow of Ulysses*, exh. 1768
To stave off having to choose between the suitors who besieged her after her husband Ulysses's purported death, Penelope took down his bow and promised to marry whoever could emulate his feat of shooting an arrow between twelve axe-rings placed in a row. Pendant to no. 105.

103 *Woman in Neapolitan Dress*
Probably painted after Kauffman's return to Italy in 1782.

105 *Venus directing Aeneas and Achates to Carthage*, exh. 1768
Aeneas and his faithful companion land on the coast of Carthage after a storm and are directed by his mother Venus towards the city of Queen Dido, with whom Aeneas is to have a tragic love affair. Pendant to no. 100.

IN HALL:

234 Manner of ENOCH SEEMAN
(1689/90–1744/5)
Lady Catherine Parker (1706–58)
The second daughter of the 1st Earl Poulett, she married John Parker in 1725. Her money helped to pay for rebuilding Saltram in the 1740s.

99 After RAPHAEL (1483–1520)
The Triumph of Galatea
A copy of Raphael's fresco in the Villa Farnesina, Rome.

SCULPTURE

IN STAIRWELL:

Marble bust of the Emperor Augustus.

FURNITURE

Circular mahogany rent-table, with alphabetically lettered drawers and cupboard base, *c*.1810.

Italian giltwood side-table, attributed to Domenico Parodi (1688–1740).

Set of mid-eighteenth-century armchairs with original *gros* and *petit point* needlework upholstery.

ON EAST WALL:

Bracket clock, with strike and chime movement by Benjamin Gray and Justin Vulliamy, in an earlier, ormolu-mounted Boullework case. Gray was clockmaker to George II.

ON LANDING AT TOP OF STAIRS:

Pair of mahogany card-tables, *c*.1770.

Pair of mahogany pedestals carved with rams' heads, *paterae* and acanthus foliage, *c*.1770, adapted later for gas lights. (The hooks for the smoke caps can still be seen in the cornice above.)

ON STAIRS:

Frankfurt faience vase decorated in blue with Chinese figures, *c*.1680.

Turn right at the foot of the stairs into the South Corridor. On the wall of the corridor is a map of the estate dating from the second half of the 19th century. Turn right into the West Corridor

THE WEST CORRIDOR

PICTURES

The illuminated addresses mark the coming-of-age and safe return from war of members of the family in the late nineteenth and early twentieth centuries.

CERAMICS

The cabinets to the left contain eighteenth-century Chinese export dinner services.

Look through the windows to the Tudor Courtyard

THE TUDOR COURTYARD

In the eighteenth century this central courtyard would not have been seen by important visitors to Saltram. Today, it provides a fascinating glimpse of the architectural development of the house. On the left, the wall is crowded with windows of different sizes and styles, installed over the years with scant regard for symmetry. To the right, the seventeenth-century 'Bagg' tower dominates the roofscape. The walls in between bear evidence of the removal of walls and the blocking up of doorways.

THE GARDEN ROOM

In the nineteenth century this was the billiard-room, and it later became the 4th Earl's study. Now it is used by the Trust to display the collection of topographical paintings relating to Saltram, which had previously been grouped upstairs in the Southern Bow and Eastern Gallery. Together, the pictures depict the views out from the estate in the late 18th or early 19th centuries.

CHIMNEYPIECE

The chimneypiece, attributed to Thomas Carter the Younger, has a relief depicting Romulus and Remus.

PICTURES

WINDOW WALL:

JOHN NOST SARTORIUS (1759–1828)
159 *'Anvil'*, 1783

The horse was sold by Lord Boringdon to the Prince of Wales in 1784.

160 *'Saltram'*, 1783
Sired by 'Eclipse' and winner of the 1783 Derby for Lord Boringdon.

CHIMNEYPIECE WALL:

161 PHILIP HUTCHINGS ROGERS (1794–1853)
Saltram from the South-West
Painted before the south porch was added by John Foulston in 1820.

162 EDMUND GARVEY, RA (c.1740/45–1813)
View near Crabtree Limekilns

163 WILLIAM TOMKINS, ARA (c.1732–92)
Distant view of Saltram, ?1779
Seen from the south-east, apparently on the high ground overlooking the park, between Stag Lodge and Wixenford Farm.

Two early eighteenth-century Chinese Mazarine blue and gilt porcelain vases (Garden Room)

164 PHILIP HUTCHINGS ROGERS (1794–1853)
Saltram from the North-East
Painted from about halfway up the Merafield drive, with the River Plym in the background.

165 EDMUND GARVEY, RA (c.1740/5–1813)
View of Crabtree Limekilns and part of Saltram
The Plym looking downstream; Crabtree Cottage and Limekilns on the right, Saltram Wood on the left, above which rises the castellated top of the Castle in the garden.

LONG WALL:

WILLIAM TOMKINS, ARA (c.1732–92)

There are seven pictures by this itinerant and much-employed painter of country seats at Saltram today.

166 *The River Plym and Saltram Wood*, 1771
Looking downstream, with Saltram Wood and the Amphitheatre on the left. The house and grounds lie behind.

167 *Mount Edgcumbe and Plymouth Sound from Saltram*
Almost the same view as no. 139. The Citadel at Plymouth can clearly be seen in the middle distance, with Mount Edgcumbe House on the right of it in the background.

168 *The Amphitheatre at Saltram*, 1770
Looking upstream, with Saltram Wood on the right. Lord Boringdon's private barge conveys a visiting party to Blaxton Quay, while a salute is fired from the Amphitheatre cannon. The façade of the classical Amphitheatre, which was almost certainly erected by John Parker, survives. The statue and cannons have gone, but the French hunting horns are displayed over the door to the West Corridor.

SHORT WALL:

169 BRITISH SCHOOL, nineteenth-century
The Flying Bridge Ferry across the Laira
Replaced by the 1st Earl in 1824 with the cast-iron bridge designed by J. M. Rendel, which was itself demolished in 1961.

170 AMBROSE BOWDEN JOHNS (1776–1858)
Plym Bridge, near Boringdon Woods

171 BRITISH SCHOOL, late-eighteenth century
Unidentified river view

172 WILLIAM TOMKINS, ARA (c.1732–92)
Plymouth, Mount Edgcumbe, and Plymouth Sound, from Saltram

Mount Edgcumbe is the wooded height in the background.

FURNITURE

IN CENTRE OF ROOM:

Regency mahogany library table from Stourhead. On top is a glass case made at Saltram for temporary exhibition of books and archives.

FLANKING CHIMNEYPIECE:

Pair of satinwood Pembroke tables by Henry Kettle (active 1777–96)

EAST WALL:

Fall-front escritoire (writing-desk) veneered in burr walnut over an oak carcase, late seventeenth-century.

Pair of side-tables with black painted frames and inlaid Florentine marble tops, c.1768.

BETWEEN WINDOWS:

Pair of early eighteenth-century Italian giltwood side-tables with shaped marble tops.

CERAMICS

DISPLAYED THROUGHOUT ROOM:

A collection of Chinese Mazarine blue and gilt porcelain vases, early eighteenth-century.

OTHER

SOUTH WALL:

Flintlock musketoon made for Lord Boringdon by H. Hadley of London (active 1734–73) with silver mounts, hallmarked London 1762/3, probably by J. Ashley. Designed for firing from horseback, as a defence against highwaymen when travelling.

Two French flintlock double-barrelled pistols, c.1770.

Double-barrelled flintlock pistol made by Tate, c.1780.

OVER DOOR TO WEST CORRIDOR:

Two French hunting horns by John Christopher Hofmaster (active 1751–63) and Nicholas Winkings (active 1735–63); see no. 135. They may have been the French horns referred to by Theresa Parker in 1769 as 'playing all dinner time and again in the wood in the evening' to herald her arrival at Saltram as Lord Boringdon's wife.

THE MIRROR ROOM

In the eighteenth century this was a vestibule containing a staircase to the first floor. The staircase has long since gone, and the Trust has decorated the room with Chinese 'factory' wallpaper depicting scenes from daily life, transferred from another room not open to visitors. The Chinese mirror paintings, from which the room takes its name, are mid–eighteenth-century. Five have contemporary English Rococo giltwood frames; the others retain their original black and gold lacquer frames.

The Venetian window, squashed asymmetrically into one corner of the room, suggests that the architect was working to a limited budget.

CHIMNEYPIECE

The mid-eighteenth-century chimneypiece is similar to that in the Stone Hall at Uppark.

FURNITURE

IN CENTRE OF ROOM:

Regency circular rosewood library table with gilt brass mounts, by J. McLane & Son.

The Mirror Room

Four 'Chinese Chippendale' mahogany chairs, eighteenth-century.

RIGHT OF FIREPLACE:

Padoukwood card- or tea-table with a circular folding top and apron inlaid with mother-of-pearl. Possibly made in the East Indies to an early eighteenth-century English design.

ON SOUTH WALL:

Chippendale mahogany card table with a pierced apron to the front and sides. English, 1760–80.

Two mid-eighteenth-century padoukwood chairs with fretwork backs and pagoda-shaped cresting rails, part of the set from the Chinese Chippendale Bedroom.

BETWEEN WINDOWS:

Early eighteenth-century giltwood side-table with Chinese lacquer top.

A Derby white sauceboat, c.1750–55 (Mirror Room)

CERAMICS

Some of the finest pieces from Saltram's outstanding ceramics collection are displayed here. A full list is available in the room.

PIECES IN CABINET INCLUDE:

BOTH SIDES, SECOND SHELF FROM TOP:

Worcester tea or coffee service, enamelled in London in the workshop of James Giles, *c.*1770.

LEFT-HAND SIDE, FOURTH SHELF FROM TOP:

Six Meissen porcelain cats and kittens, *c.*1736–45.

RIGHT-HAND SIDE, FOURTH SHELF FROM TOP:

Two Plymouth bell-shaped mugs painted with 'Soqui Birds', *c.*1770.

Pair of Plymouth salts in the form of shells, *c.*1770.

Set of four Plymouth white figures of children symbolising the Seasons, *c.*1770.

Plymouth white sweetmeat stand in the form of three fluted shells set on shell- and coral-work, *c.*1770.

Derby white sauceboat in the form of a shell, *c.*1750–55.

A mid-eighteenth-century Chinese mirror painting in an English Rococo frame of the same date

THE LIBRARY

The evolution of the Library reflects the rising status of such rooms in the houses of the wealthy. In the mid-eighteenth century, there were two rooms here, separated by a wall where the scagliola columns are now. The near room was an eating-room, which became a Library, when Adam's library was transformed into the Dining Room in 1778. At the end of the eighteenth century, new book presses were set into the walls, as the 1st Earl's sister described:

The Library is wonderfully improved and the difference of the size is greater than I supposed it would be. The bookcases being mahogany will look dark, I think, when they grow old, but at present they look very well indeed, and the room is extremely pretty.

The collection of Books is considerably improved, not without reason to be sure.

The bow end was a drawing-room, which was often used for musical entertainment in the 1st Earl's time. The Rev. Talbot recalled one occasion in 1811:

Every Evg. Ld. B. calls for a little Music, & [the Countess] has perhaps a little improved herself in it – her stock seems to be an infinite Variety of Waltzes with the Music of all the operas that come out, & she keeps up singing enough to set every Body going that have any Disposition that Way.

The present appearance of the Library dates from 1819, when the 1st Earl employed the architect John Foulston to combine the drawing-room and library as one large room. At the same time, he installed

The Library

the white marble chimneypieces and overmantel mirrors, which had probably been purchased on the family's trip to France in 1818. The cornices and pediments were added to the book presses in the early twentieth century.

BOOKS

Most of the books date from the 1st Earl's time. The Rev. Talbot called them 'the finest Classics I ever saw, a large collection of fine Books of Prints of all kinds and a very large collection of original Drawings of the Old Masters of the different Schools.'

PICTURES

Bust- or half-length portraits were a traditional adornment to a library, conveniently filling the space between the tops of the bookshelves and the ceiling. Since the early nineteenth century, portraits by Reynolds, Kauffman, and later those by Gilbert Stuart, have been concentrated here.

NEAR CHIMNEYPIECE WALL, LEFT TO RIGHT:

SIR JOSHUA REYNOLDS, PRA (1723–92)
69 *John Parker* (1703–68), 1767
Although inscribed as of Lord Boringdon, actually a portrait of his father, who remodelled Saltram in the 1740s.

70 *Sir John Chichester, 5th Bt* (1721–84), 1767
From an old north Devon family, who lived at Raleigh. In 1773 Theresa Parker called him 'such a log of wood'.

71 *Commodore Harrison, c.1767–8*
Probably a friend of Lord Boringdon, whom he may have met while serving with the fleet at Plymouth.

72 *Walter Radcliffe* (1733–1803), 1757–61
A friend and neighbour of Lord Boringdon. In 1772 Theresa thought him 'grown more reasonable, and will sometimes prefer a good House and good company to being alone at Warleigh [his home near Plymouth] for more than two days following without much pressing'.

ENTRANCE (HALL) WALL, LEFT TO RIGHT:

JAMES NORTHCOTE, RA (1746–1831)
73 *Admiral Sir Hyde Parker, 5th Bt* (1714–82), 1781
A distinguished sailor, and a distant relative of the Parkers of Saltram.

74 *John Arscott* (d.1788)
The epitome of the old-fashioned squire, and the last private gentleman to keep a jester, Black John, whose special tricks were swallowing mice and sparrow-mumbling.

75 Studio of SIR JOSHUA REYNOLDS, PRA (1723–92)
Sir Charles Davers, 6th Bt, MP (1737–1806)
Of Rushbrooke, Bury St Edmunds. MP for the town, 1774–1802.

WINDOW WALL, LEFT TO RIGHT:

ANGELICA KAUFFMAN, RA (1741–1807)
58 *John Parker, later 1st Lord Boringdon* (1734/5–88)
Painted while on his honeymoon Grand Tour with his first wife, Frances Hort. He is wearing powdered hair, unlike in the Reynolds portrait of him (no. 29; Morning Room).

59 *Self-portrait of the Artist*
Probably painted in Italy and acquired by Lord Boringdon while on his Grand Tour. Badly damaged.

GILBERT STUART (1755–1828)
This American-born artist is best known for his much-reproduced portraits of George Washington.

60 *John, 1st Earl of Morley* (1772–1840) *as a Boy*
Probably painted when he left Westminster School.

BEYOND COLUMNS, CLOCKWISE FROM LEFT OF WINDOW BAY:

65 *Thomas (Robinson), 2nd Baron Grantham* (1738–86)
Brother of Theresa Parker. Ambassador in Madrid (1771–9) and Foreign Secretary (1782–3). Commissioned by Lord Boringdon in 1784.

66 *Richard Coffin* (d.1796), 1778?
Richard Bennett assumed the name Coffin on inheriting his uncle's Portledge estate in Devon in 1766.

67 *John, 1st Earl of Morley* (1772–1840) *as a Boy, c.1781*

68 *Admiral Sir Charles Pole, Bt* (1757–1830)
Younger brother of Reginald Pole-Carew of Antony (also NT). He lived in Devon, becoming MP for Plymouth in 1806.

61 *Sir John Hort, 1st Bt* (1735–1807)
Brother of Lord Boringdon's first wife, Frances Hort. Consul in Lisbon, 1767–98.

The 1st Earl of Morley (1772–1840) as a Boy; by Gilbert Stuart, c.1781 (no. 117; Library)

62 *Thomas (Pelham), 2nd Earl of Chichester* (1756–1826)
Irish Secretary (1795–8), Home Secretary (1801–3) and Postmaster-General (1807–26). Theresa Parker referred to his 'jockey-coxcombe antics'.

63 *The Hon. Samuel Barrington* (1729–1800)
Entered the Navy in 1741 and was made admiral in 1787. He had a reputation in the service for kind-heartedness and humanity.

64 *The Hon. Frederick Robinson* (1746–92)
Younger brother of Theresa Parker, who wrote many letters about Saltram to her as 'Fritz'.

FURNITURE

Boulle writing-desk. According to family tradition, this desk was given by Louis XIV to Sarah, Duchess of Marlborough, who gave it to her granddaughter Mary, Duchess of Montagu, who in turn gave it to Lady Catherine Parker. (The Duchess of Montagu was godmother to Montagu Parker, Lady Catherine's younger son.) It is of beechwood inlaid with brass and shell, and is thought to be by the great French cabinetmaker André-Charles Boulle (1642–1732). The decoration is in the manner of Jean Bérain, who helped to create the Louis XIV style, and the details in the corners depict four figures with the attendant animals associated with the four known Continents: crocodile – America; lion – Africa; white horse – Europe; camel – Asia. Unfortunately, the desk was restored rather clumsily in the nineteenth century, when the leather panel in the top was added.

ON BOULLE DESK:

Silver-gilt inkstand, made in Madrid in 1779, and designed for Theresa's elder brother, Thomas (a drawing for it is on display in the East Corridor).

Regency rosewood games-table with cross-over legs painted to simulate bronze, and made by the London firm J. McLane & Son (active 1770–1815). The middle section of the top is reversible and is fitted with a backgammon board.

Mahogany library chair, on which the reader sits back to front, to face their book propped on an adjustable rest, *c*.1805.

Set of Regency mahogany library steps which folds up to form a sabre-leg armchair – the 'Patent Meta-morphic Library Chair' by Morgan and Sanders.

Set of mahogany-framed chairs, two stamped 'P. Bellangé' – Pierre Antoine Bellangé (1758–1837), *ébéniste* to Louis XVIII. Probably purchased by the 1st Earl and Countess in France, 1817–18.

Burr yew-wood writing-table with lyre-shaped supports, *c*.1800.

CERAMICS

Pair of black basalt ware vases, Wedgwood & Bentley, *c*.1770–5.

Four engine-turned Wedgwood cream-coloured earthenware vases and covers, *c*.1765.

Four Wedgwood & Bentley black basalt ware vases, *c*.1770–5.

CLOCKS

ON CHIMNEYPIECES:

Pair of early nineteenth-century eight-day clocks by Le Roy of Paris.

The tour ends in the Entrance Hall.

SALTRAM AND ITS OWNERS

Saltram takes its name from the salt that was har-vested from a nearby salt marsh on the tidal estuary of the River Plym. (Salt was an important food preservative.) The suffix indicates that there was a 'ham', or homestead, on the site before the Tudor period.

The first family associated with Saltram were the Mayhowes or Mayes, who were yeoman farmers here in the sixteenth century. They owned Saltram for about 50 years, their prosperity declining only at the end of the century, when they began to sell or lease parts of the estate. Their holdings were clearly considerable; a lease of 1588 granted the right to farm in Saltram Wood 'and all houses, quays and buildings adjoining or upon the same', and to have fishing rights at Laira Prince Rock and Culverhole; to hold portions of a quay called Coldharbour; and to have the use of the Mayhowes' fishing nets. Today, Saltram still preserves elements of the Mayhowes' farmhouse, notably their kitchen and what was probably a shippon (now the Chapel).

The next family known to have owned Saltram were the Baggs, who were probably responsible for turning the farmhouse into a mansion. Sir James Bagg, son of George Bagg of Weymouth, moved to Plymouth some time before 1590, and purchased the farm at Saltram in about 1614. He held the offices of agent for the Crown, Collector of Customs for Plymouth and Fowey, MP for Plymouth, and Mayor for the city in 1595 and 1605–6. He was known as an ambitious and unscrupulous man, in 1613 calling a local dignitary 'an insolent knave' and threatening to break the neck of another. On his death in 1624, his will stated:

To my wife, four chambers in my dwelling house in Plymouth [Saltram]. That is to saye, the Chamber where I doe usually lye in. The Chamber next without it. The Porch Chamber and the Chamber wheare my Servantmaids doe lye in, for and during the terme of her life or so long as she shall either by her self or with the Children inhabit and live in them with free egress and regress to the house ... Also to my wife – the sum of £30 or value of the same in household goods.

Saltram passed to Sir James's son, also called James, who quickly surpassed his father in notoriety. He has been described as 'spectacularly obsequious ... the worst type of corrupt, court-backed local tyrant', and a man who was 'prepared to go to almost any length in his quest for personal power and wealth'. He was one of two vice-admirals responsible for the southern shore of Cornwall, and closely allied to James I's favourite, the Duke of Buckingham, who often stayed at Saltram. On Charles I's accession in 1625, Buckingham persuaded the King to launch an attack on the Spanish at Cadiz. Bagg was appointed prestmaster (responsible for the press-gang) and victualler for the expedition which was to set off from Plymouth, and was knighted when Charles I came to visit the troops. The expedition failed, partly because Bagg embezzled the £55,000 given to him to purchase provisions for the King's ships, supplying the fleet instead with cheap, rotten food which had 'killed four thousand of the King's Subjects'. To pay for the rotten food, Bagg had even run up debts in the King's name. Surprisingly, the King defended Bagg against his accusers. When a second embezzlement charge was brought, and the King again defended Bagg, Archbishop Laud was prompted to proclaim: 'I have now done with that bottomless bag.'

Bagg died a disgraced debtor in 1638, and most of his property, Saltram excepted, was immediately seized by the Crown. At this time Saltram was described as comprising: 'One great mansion house, one stable, one shipping, one piggion house, three gardens, two acrs of orchards, eight acrs of meadows, thirty two acrs of pasture land, fiftee foure acrs of arable land and one acre of Coppies Woods.' The same document lists 85 properties in the surrounding area which were also part of the Saltram estate at that time. An illustrated map of 1643 suggests that the Baggs' 'great mansion house' was a three-storey building, with a hipped roof and two large gables, and judging by the physical remains of this house, it was constructed around a central courtyard. The most prominent survival is the staircase tower which forms the south-east corner of the Tudor courtyard.

James Bagg's son, George, inherited his father's debts and the Deputy Governorship of Plymouth. In 1642 the English Civil War broke out, and over several years took its toll on Saltram, as George Bagg later complained: 'The orchards, gardens and

woods are all spoyled and cutt downe and distroyed and I make no proffit thereof.' Bagg was a Royalist, and when the war ended, he had to pay the Commonwealth government £582 to secure his estates. Having held on to Saltram for the duration of the war, the Baggs lost it for good in 1660, when it was transferred to Captain Henry Hatsell by the Government, in lieu of the large Government debt owed to him. Hatsell was a Parliamentarian, and customs officer for Plymouth, who became MP for Devon and then Vice-Admiral of the county. After the Restoration in 1660, Saltram passed by Royal Charter to Sir George Carteret, as repayment for the large sum of money he had loaned the King during the Civil War.

In 1712 Saltram was purchased by George Parker of North Molton and Boringdon, both also in Devon. The history of the Parkers before this date is uncertain, but according to the 3rd Earl's account of the family, they were living at North Molton from 1320. Boringdon, only two miles north of Saltram, belonged to the family from 1583 until the 1920s; the surviving wing is now a hotel. The traveller Celia Fiennes described the house at Saltram in 1698:

Two mile from Plymouth we come to the river Plym just by a little town [Plympton] all built of stone and the tyleing is all slatt, which with the lime its cemented with makes it look white like snow, and in the sun shineing on the slatt it glisters; here I came in sight on the right hand of a very large house [Saltram] built all with this sort of stone which is a sort of marble; this house look'd very finely in a thicket of trees like a grove and was on the side of a hill, and led just down to the head of the river Plym which is fill'd with the tyde from the sea.

It seems that George Parker never lived at Saltram, which was let for his lifetime to Thomas Wolstenholme. He also purchased the Whiteway estate, near Chudleigh, and Polsloe Priory, on the edge of Exeter. On his death in 1743, Saltram passed to John Parker, his son by his second marriage.

(Left) The internal courtyard preserves fragments of Tudor Saltram and the tower built by the Bagg family in the seventeenth century

JOHN PARKER
(1703–68)

In 1725 John Parker married Lady Catherine Poulett, daughter of the 1st Earl Poulett, Secretary of State and Lord Steward to Queen Anne. This was an excellent match for a country squire, which enhanced the family's social status. To begin with, John Parker and Lady Catherine were clearly undecided as to where best to make their home. At first Boringdon was preferred: there were plans for remodelling the house and creating an elaborate garden. Family tradition maintains that John Parker laid the foundations for these additions, but then fell seriously ill, and his wife started work to turn Saltram into her dower-house. Having recovered unexpectedly, John Parker abandoned plans for Boringdon and continued Lady Catherine's expansion of Saltram.

Whatever the truth of the matter, several drawings indicate that the Parkers' plans were always ambitious. They commissioned a design from William Kent, a leading exponent of Palladianism,

Lady Catherine Parker (1706–58), whose money helped to pay for the rebuilding of Saltram in the 1740s; attributed to Enoch Seeman (no. 234; Staircase Hall)

which sought a return to the purer form of classical architecture established by the Italian architect Andrea Palladio (1508–80). If Kent's house had been built, 'it would have rivalled Holkham'. Another drawing (illustrated on p. 44 and now hanging in the East Corridor) is inscribed 'To the Rt Hon the Lady Katharine Parker at Saltram', giving rise to the family tradition that she supervised the building work herself. If this house had been built, it would have had a façade at least 370 feet in length.

In comparison with these grand proposals, the work which was actually carried out in the 1740s was modest. To save money, three classical façades, all different, were loosely wrapped around the existing buildings. This can be seen best at the corner of the west and south fronts, which are remarkably at odds with one another for a house of Saltram's importance. The south front has a pedimented central block and flanking bays, all of three storeys. The east front comprises a three-storey central block stepped forward between two pedi-

John Parker (1703–68); by Sir Joshua Reynolds (no. 69; Library)

The Chinese mirror paintings and wallpapers were introduced by John and Lady Catherine Parker

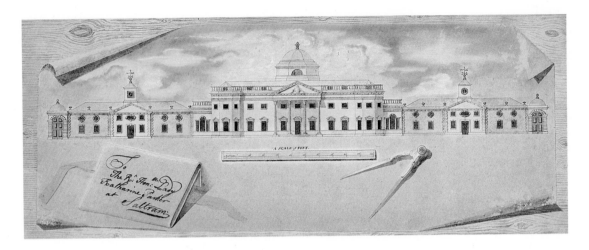

Lady Catherine seems to have commissioned this design for a great house. The Parkers eventually decided on a more modest remodelling of Saltram (East Corridor)

mented wings of the same height, and the whole façade is dominated by the great Venetian window of the Saloon. Two more Venetian windows, coupled with therm windows, appear in the low wings that join the central block of the west front to the pavilions. Little attention was paid to making the internal layout correspond with the exterior. This is particularly apparent on the west front, where the new façade has been built in front of the older structure, with false windows and a false door to achieve symmetry in a Palladian pattern of 2-3-5-3-2 windows. To give the west front added weight, four copies of Graeco-Roman statues, probably by John Cheere, were put up in the pavilion niches. None of this properly screens the earlier building, which is visible beyond the irregular roofline. The architect of the 1740s house has not yet been identified, but suggestions range from a London-based architect to a West Country imitator of Lord Burlington's circle.

In contrast with the exterior, the interior of the Parkers' house shows little evidence of economising. Their plasterwork and joinery in the main rooms is of high quality, and subsequent generations of the family were happy to incorporate it in updated decorative schemes, rather than starting anew. Little of the present contents can be con-

fidently attributed to John and Lady Catherine Parker, but a few pieces stand out. One is Lady Catherine's Boulle desk, said to have been made for Louis XIV, and now in the Library. John and Lady Catherine probably also introduced the astonishing collection of Chinese wallpapers. Saltram originally had at least four rooms decorated with Chinese wallpaper – one of the most expensive components of the Chinoiserie style, which was at its height from around 1740 to 1790. Remarkably, the Saltram wallpapers represent almost every stylistic variation of the medium. They cost between four and seven shillings a yard, at a time when housemaids were paid between £4 and £8 a year.

Family tradition also maintains that Lady Catherine indirectly initiated Saltram's great art collection. Sir Joshua Reynolds was born in the neighbouring parish of Plympton St Maurice in 1723, where his father was the master of the local grammar school. Reynolds became friends with the Parker family, and Lady Catherine is said to have given him his first drawing pencil. He later became the most important British artist of his day, and the first President of the Royal Academy.

Lady Catherine died in 1758, but improvements at Saltram continued. A new room was begun – the Saloon – the same height as the Staircase Hall, and with a similar deep cove. Fifty feet in length, and 25 feet in breadth and height, its shape was a double cube – a form made fashionable by Inigo Jones at Wilton House. A large Venetian window was inserted in the east wall, and the chimneypiece, by Thomas Carter the Younger, may also date from this time, since his was one of the last bills that John Parker paid before he died in 1768, leaving the new room unfinished. Parker's legacy to his son was the inspiration to embellish Saltram in a grand manner, and the means to do this. At his death, more than £32,000 was found hidden about the house: '... cash in bags placed in the mahogany book case £3717; ditto placed in the wainscott toilet £3928.'

JOHN PARKER, 1ST LORD BORINGDON
(1734/5–88)

John Parker was educated at Christ Church, Oxford, where he became firm friends with the Earl of Shelburne, a future Prime Minister who secured him a seat in Parliament, as MP for Bodmin in 1761, and Devon in 1762. However, Lord Boringdon was far more interested in shooting, horse-racing and gambling than in a political career. The portrait of him by Reynolds in the Morning Room depicts a country squire leaning against a gate with a shotgun over his arm, and his account books record large sums won and lost at the races and at cards. On one visit to Saltram, the Duchess of Devonshire, who was an equally avid gambler, described him as being 'as dirty, as comical, and talking as bad English as ever'.

Like most young men of good family at the time, Lord Boringdon was expected to embark on a Grand Tour as part of his education. In 1764 he travelled to Italy with his new bride, Frances Hort, a cousin of Lord Shelburne, but she fell ill and died in Naples later that year. Lord Boringdon's second marriage was the decisive factor in the development of Saltram. His choice was the Hon. Theresa Robinson, daughter of the 1st Lord Grantham, and god-daughter of the Empress Maria Theresa of Austria, after whom she was named. Just as for his father, marriage raised the young John Parker to a higher rank in society, and in 1784 he was created Baron Boringdon – a title befitting his wealth, and the status he acquired through his wife. For Theresa, the marriage brought financial security; despite their social position, the Robinsons were not rich.

If Theresa's family had any doubts about her moving to Devon, far from the polite society of London, they must have been reassured by her first letter from Saltram, written two weeks after her wedding in 1769: 'I could not help thinking how happy you would all have been to have seen the manner in which I was entertained, French horns playing all dinner time and again in the wood in the evening when the guns were fired but I will not say any more about it, as Mr. Parker will very likely see this letter and may fancy I am complimenting him.' Theresa came from a sophisticated, cultured background. Her elder brother, Thomas, 2nd Lord

John Parker, 1st Lord Boringdon (1734/5–88); by Joshua Reynolds (no. 29; Morning Room). Reynolds was born near Saltram and generously supported by the Parkers

Grantham, was an amateur architect and member of the Society of Dilettanti. Theresa, though perfectly capable herself in such matters, clearly relied on him for help with furnishing Saltram, and in 1771 she wrote: 'remember that if you meet with anything abroad, of pictures bronzes etc. that is valuable in itself, beautiful and proper for any part of Saltram we depend so much upon your taste and judgement that you must not lose an opportunity of procuring it for us.' Theresa's younger brother, Frederick (known as Fritz), and her sister, Anne (known as Nanny), were equally discerning, and all four kept up a regular correspondence which records the rapidly changing appearance of Saltram in the 1770s. Writing in 1774 from Madrid, where Thomas was British Ambassador, Fritz addressed a sonnet to Nanny, which underlines how important matters of taste were to the family:

Had I my Brothers Art divine
Of drawing frames in pen and ink
Could I write Sonnets smooth and fine
And say in verse whate'er I think
Here might you see how both our faces
Are set in frames of black and gold
Like China Gods in Japan cases
To Dowagers at Auctions sold
Then would you know I love you more
Than I am able to express
And tho' upon a distant shore
Shall never, *never* love you less
I too an altar would attempt to raise
And in harmonious numbers sing your praise.

In 1768, the year he inherited Saltram, Lord Boringdon commissioned Robert Adam to improve the house with the very latest thing in interior design. At the time, Adam was the most fashionable architect in England, with Harewood House, Croome Court, Kedleston Hall, Syon House and Osterley Park already among his commissions, as well as work for Lord Shelburne at Bowood and Lansdowne House. In *The Works in Architecture* (1773) Adam contrasted the Palladian style of the previous 30 years – 'the massive entablature, the ponderous compartment ceiling, the tabernacle frame' – with his own approach – 'a beautiful variety of light mouldings, gracefully formed, delicately enriched and arranged with propriety and skill'. Another aspect of the Adam style was the rejection of the traditional white ceiling in favour of pastel-tinted backgrounds. He was also innovative in designing everything himself, from ceilings to doorknobs and furniture, in order to achieve a new consistency in style.

Many of Adam's clients asked him to design interiors for an existing house, rather than building anew, and this was the brief at Saltram. Like his parents, Lord Boringdon wanted to preserve much of the earlier structure, including his mother's Palladian and Rococo work, as his brother-in-law noted in 1769: 'the two new rooms [Saloon and Library] are very forward, they are highly finished . . . the Stucco in the other parts of the house

Theresa Parker (1744/5–75); by Joshua Reynolds, 1770–72 (no. 76; Saloon)

The Wedgwood earthenware vases in the Library were probably bought by Theresa

is not in a good taste but still much too good to destroy'.

Between 1768 and 1772 Adam completed the Saloon, begun by Lord Boringdon's father, and created an adjoining Library (now the Dining Room). The Saloon is still very much as it was in the eighteenth century, but Adam's library has been considerably altered. The latter originally had pale green walls, stone-coloured mouldings, a lilac ground to the frieze, red draperies, and stucco medallions painted blue and white like Wedgwood ware – an interesting colour scheme, which perhaps explains Fritz's reaction in 1770: 'There is no describing the library, it is fitted up like a snuff box, they do not live in [it] yet because of the noise of the workmen in the next room [the Saloon]. There are more books than I thought.' To provide a fitting entrance to the new Saloon, Adam also designed the pair of gilt mirrors and tables which flank the doorway at the Saloon end of the Velvet Drawing Room. In the same period, he produced designs for a pair of lodge buildings at the main entrance to the park, and a drawing-room ceiling for the Parkers'

London house. In 1772 Theresa wrote to Fritz, 'All our building draws very near a conclusion. A new Eating Room ... is thought of at a distance, but if we leave nothing for the little boy to do, he will certainly pull to pieces what we have done, or perhaps wonder how money could be laid out at Saltram and go and build at Boringdon.'

Theresa played an active part in all the improvements at Saltram, including the choice of works of art and furnishings – a matter then usually reserved for men. Only four months after her arrival at Saltram, she wrote to Fritz asking him 'to call at Zucchi's and let us have your opinion on the paintings he has finished for the Library' and 'to send some patterns of Blue Damask, as we shall soon write to Genoa and wish to fix upon the best Blue for setting off the Pictures'. And it was not just the grand rooms which required careful thought; Theresa chose 'some of Wedgwood's best unglazed ware' for her dressing-room, since she considered unglazed ceramics of this kind to be 'the only ornamental ware'. Theresa was also an artist and designer in her own right. In 1772 her elder brother wrote to Nanny about Theresa's design for an inkstand: 'I am delighted with her Design, and am choaking with Jealousy and Admiration of it.' She had ample time to indulge these interests, as in London her husband often left her on her own for the evening, while he attended late parliamentary sittings and played cards at Boodle's.

The picture collection at Saltram is of outstanding quality for two reasons. Firstly, because Lord Boringdon had access to the finest artists of the day, and secondly because his wife and her family had excellent judgement in such matters. Reynolds was a family friend, who regularly visited Saltram, shot on the estate, and often gambled with Lord Boringdon. After Theresa's arrival, however, the name 'Parker', and later 'Boringdon', features in Reynolds's pocket books more frequently than that of any other sitter. There are eleven portraits by him at Saltram, and he also advised the family on buying pictures by other artists for the collection. A correction in a letter from Theresa to her elder brother about her half-length portrait shows that she, rather than her husband, was the decision-maker in these matters: 'I have some thoughts (that is) Mr. Parker

Joshua Reynolds; by Angelica Kauffman, 1767 (no. 107; Staircase Hall)

talks, of having the little Boy [their son] put into the half length at Sir Joshua's which remains just as you left it, only in bright yellow, which he is very fond of at present but I do not approve of.'

Lord Boringdon had already sat to Angelica Kauffman while in Naples on his Grand Tour in 1764, two years before she moved to Britain under the patronage of Lady Wentworth. There are twelve paintings by Kauffman at Saltram, including the set of four history paintings intended for the Saloon, and she also supplied a collection of Old Master drawings (now in the Library), of the sort acquired by wealthy Englishmen on the Grand Tour. In 1775, Fritz wrote enquiring about Kauffman's pictures at Saltram – Theresa, as usual, was ready with an opinion: 'The prettiest and I think the best she ever did is the painting of Hector and Andromache' (now in the Staircase Hall).

Theresa Parker had two children. John, the future 1st Earl of Morley, was born in 1772; his sister, Theresa, arrived three years later. Soon after the birth of her second child, Theresa became ill and

died, aged 31. Reynolds paid tribute to her as a woman of 'skill and exact judgment in the fine arts' who 'seemed to possess by a kind of intuition that propriety of taste and right thinking which others but imperfectly acquire by long labour and application'. The children were left in the care of their aunt, Nanny, who lived at Saltram for the next twenty years, at different times fulfilling the roles of mother, hostess and estate manager, and overseeing a house staff which comprised housekeeper, two housemaids, kitchenmaid, still-room maid, scullery maid, laundry maid, cook, brewer, two footmen, butler, under-butler and governess. In doing so, she gave up any hopes she had of a good marriage, and accepted a life of financial dependency on her brother-in-law.

Theresa's death did not stop the building activity at Saltram. In 1778 a fire destroyed the laundry and brew-house, giving Lord Boringdon the excuse for a major reorganisation of the service areas. Nanny hoped that her brother, Lord Grantham, would be asked 'to plan and contrive it for the best', but Lord Boringdon turned again to his favourite architect. Adam produced a grand scheme to create a comprehensive service area to the north, and a spectacular, circular dining-room with apses, niches and a semicircular portico in the middle of the west front. The new dining-room was to be linked to the Saloon and its adjoining rooms by a niche-lined gallery, 71 feet long, and the servants' hall was to be relocated for practicality at the heart of the house. Unfortunately, Adam's plans were too ambitious for Lord Boringdon, who decided to rely instead on the skills of his estate carpenter, Henry Stockman. The laundry and brew-house were rebuilt as a separate block north of the house, and a new kitchen constructed of brick to a design by Stockman and Thomas Parlby, the chief builder of the Plymouth Docks. The new kitchen was at the opposite end of the house from the existing eating-room on the south front. The solution was to turn Adam's library into a dining-room, and move the bookcases into the old eating-room. Adam's contribution to the project was minimal, and as a result the unified quality of his earlier library scheme was lost. His last commission, in 1782, was to design a Triumphal Arch at Boringdon, which was intended to be seen from the north window of the Dining Room.

Lord Boringdon died in 1788, one year before Saltram received the ultimate social recognition – a royal visit from George III, who stayed with his entourage for several weeks. The Saltram estate steward described how the King was 'in a high good humour speaking of the beauty of the place – the different objects in view – the Lady Catherine – her manner of getting the house built'. The novelist Fanny Burney, who was a lady-in-waiting to the Queen, considered the house to be 'one of the most magnificent in the kingdom. It accommodated us all, even to every footman, without by any means filling the whole . . . I had a sweet parlour allotted to me, with the far most beautiful view of any on the ground floor, opening upon the state apartments.' Saltram also had a visit from the actress Sarah Siddons, but Nanny was unimpressed, describing her as 'very pompous and not entertaining at all'.

After Lord Boringdon's death, it was agreed that Nanny should stay on at Saltram until her nephew came of age. She had been left no money by her brother-in-law, since the estate was now in debt, but was 'perfectly satisfied with respect to my cir-cumstances, they are as much as I ever was entitled to, and I have so liberally and confidentially shared in all the Happiness, Comforts and advantages of this House and Fortune that I cannot but think myself under many and great obligations . . . As to making a more ample provision for me, you know [Lord Boringdon] could not do it without increasing your trouble and [his son's] difficulties, neither of which could have been comfortable to me.' There was plenty to occupy her time, whether it was organising the making of 'chair covers and window curtains out of the old chintzes and old stores of Lady Catherine's hoarding up', or practising 'ladies' amusements' with her young niece. Featherwork was especially popular, and often mentioned in Nanny's letters: 'We pick up every Feather that we see, and have got a great collection of them, if you want any of them or all for your panels for Mr. Cambridge's Commodes I will send them, but as I suppose you will want large ones, I don't know if they will go in a letter.' News of the French Revolution filtered through to Saltram, where the family went into mourning after the execution of Marie Antoinette, who was the daughter of Theresa Robinson's godmother.

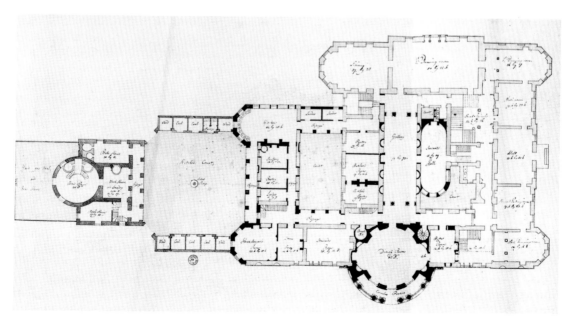

Adam's 1779 proposal included a new niche-lined sculpture gallery and circular dining-room, neither of which was built

JOHN PARKER,
1ST EARL OF MORLEY
(1772–1840)

While still a very young man, the 2nd Lord Boring-don wrote a note to his aunt Nanny which gives an insight into his character. He assured her that he 'never will make myself a fool and dupe to any such follies as perfume, dress or any such frippery. The perfume you allude to was when I left Saltram very little in quantity, and was at the end of the journey nearly gone'. Handsome and self-possessed, John, 2nd Lord Boringdon was known as 'Borino' (meaning, perhaps, 'little Boringdon'). At Oxford, he acquired an influential circle of friends, including George Canning, Lord Liverpool, Lord Granville and several others who were to become the leading politicians of their time. After university, he went into politics as a Tory, supporting some far-sighted proposals, including those for Catholic emancipa-tion, parliamentary reform and vaccination against smallpox. In spite of this, he never received a government post, although he was created Viscount Boringdon and Earl of Morley in 1815.

In 1804 he married Lady Augusta Fane, daughter of the Earl of Westmorland, but was divorced from her in 1809 after she eloped with Sir Arthur Paget. That year he wrote to his sister, Theresa Villiers, about a second potential bride, Frances Talbot: 'Her knowledge ... of painting is certainly equal to any of the London cognoscenti – she is also very fond of riding, and has some knowledge of music and singing.' But he would ask his friends for more information before making a decision:

The condition of her family, their numbers, their sanity of mind – the age of the individual about which I know nothing more than that she was grown up seven years ago, and may now by her looks be either twenty-five or forty – I shall then consider her as a very good wife in the quadruple contingency of my feeling myself disposed towards matrimony at any period – of nothing more eligible turning up in the interim, of the Lady being then unmarried, of Ditto being then willing.

Miss Talbot was willing, and they were married later that year. Those, like Lady Granville, who knew Borino were shocked: 'Were you surprised at Lord Boringdon's marriage? Miss Talbot is a most delightful person, extremely pretty and agreeable. How they all do surprise me by accepting him. His success, just as to that, is wonderful. I do not envy his wife and happy in my mind was she who ran.'

Before her marriage, Frances Talbot was already known as a society wit. She was a favourite of the playwright Sheridan, and, later, of the Rev. Sydney Smith, essayist and wit, who wrote of her:

I believe our friend Lady Morley has hit upon the right plan in dining modestly at two. When we are absorbed in side-dishes and perplexed with variety of wine, she sits among us lightly flirting with a potato, in full possession of her faculties and at liberty to make the best use of them – a liberty, it must be owned, she does not neglect, for how agreeable she is! I like Lady Morley; she is what I call 'good company'.

Her letters were full of the subjects which occupied society at that time; in 1816 she wrote to her sister-in-law: 'Thank you for all the gossip – I never did hear of such a monster as Lord Byron – really he is a disgrace to human nature.' She corresponded with Jane Austen (whose brother was chaplain to the Parker family), and was one of the twelve people chosen to receive the first copies of *Emma*. Such was her standing in literary circles that Austen's first two novels, *Sense and Sensibility* and *Pride and Prejudice*, were attributed to her, when they were initially published anonymously. But her forte was humour. She was partly responsible for the satirical *Portraits of the Spruggins Family; Arranged by Richard Suckle-thumbkin Spruggins, Esq.*, which earned her high praise: 'The comical Countess is Hogarth in petti-coats.'

Together, the 1st Earl and Countess of Morley set about establishing their presence in Devon. The 1st Earl served as Colonel of the North Devon Mili-tia, which defended the coast from French invasion. The architect of Regency Plymouth, John Foul-ston, was employed to enlarge the Library, and to design a new entrance for the house, in the Greek Revival style. During her husband's absences, the Countess began to modernise the interior of Salt-ram, introducing Regency taste with striped wall-coverings, Greek Revival furniture, and giltwood curtain poles. She also rearranged the pictures in the Library, as she explained to her husband:

The Library, c.1825; by Nicholas Condy (private collection). From left to right: the 1st Earl of Morley; his natural son, Augustus Stapleton, who managed the estate in Lord Morley's later years; Catchpole the butler, standing; Frances, Countess of Morley; and her son, Lord Boringdon

I am making a mighty revolution in the ... Library ... I have presumed to bring out all Sir Joshua's admirable portraits from their hiding place and hung them up over the book shelves – the room is more improved than anything you can imagine, and the Pictures themselves, which are really invaluable and which were before never seen or heard of, appear to the greatest advantage. This is the first great act I have performed since the commencement of my reign.

Few pictures were added to the collection during the 1st Earl's time, probably because money was needed elsewhere. Between 1788 and 1807, the 1st Earl paid off most of the debt inherited from his father by selling land in Devon and Somerset, but by 1840 had amassed a debt of £258,000 in his own name. In part, this was the result of ambitious engineering projects, encouraged by the enthusiasm of early nineteenth-century aristocrats for industrial enterprise and scientific inquiry. (Several entries in the Earl's diary refer to social gatherings where experiments in physics and chemistry were demonstrated.) In 1807 an embankment was constructed across Chelson Meadow to reclaim land from the Plym estuary, which was later used as a racecourse. The project cost the 1st Earl more than £15,000, a sum raised by mortgaging the estate; he was awarded the gold medal of the Society of Arts for his efforts. In 1824 work began on a new bridge across the Laira, which cost approximately £30,000. The existing flying-bridge ferry functioned adequately, but the 1st Earl was determined

The construction of the cast-iron Laira Bridge in 1824 was paid for by the 1st Earl and severely depleted the estate's resources

to have the very latest thing – a cast-iron bridge. When it opened in 1827, the Laira Bridge was the second largest iron structure in existence, but as its architect, J. M. Rendel, admitted: 'The expense ... was certain and considerable, whilst its returns could only be precarious.' Rendel later designed the short-lived Cann Quarry Canal, which carried slate from the Earl's quarry to the Plymouth and Dartmoor railway by means of small boats fitted with wheels.

The 1st Earl's zeal for engineering projects was not the only drain on his financial resources. He lived extravagantly, and his grandson was shocked to record that in two years he spent £3,877 more than he had earned. Some of this undoubtedly went on relationships with women other than his wives, notably Lady Elizabeth Monck, daughter of the Earl of Arran, by whom he had three sons. Surprisingly, the 1st Earl's two families seem to have been on good terms. One of his sons by Lady Elizabeth, Augustus Stapleton, became Prime Minister Canning's private secretary, and was remembered with affection by the 3rd Earl: 'He was a dear, kind old man and always remained a great friend of the family – he was one of the executors of my Father's will and during the later part of his illness and for a short time after my succession practically managed the Estate.'

Added to their financial difficulties, the Morleys suffered the loss of two children while on holiday in France in 1817–18: Henry, aged eleven; and his half-sister, Caroline, who was only four. In 1840 the 1st Earl died, leaving debts of more than a quarter of a million pounds. Frances, Countess of Morley survived her husband by seventeen years, spending much of her time at Saltram copying paintings in oil and watercolour (some of which are displayed in the Boudoir).

EDMUND PARKER, 2ND EARL OF MORLEY
(1810–64)

The life of the 2nd Earl of Morley was dominated by financial troubles. His son described him as 'a tall (6ft. 2in) active man, an excellent shot and a most amiable popular man'. In the 1840s he was a Lord-in-Waiting to Prince Albert, and later to Queen Victoria. He succeeded his father as Chairman of the Plymouth Chamber of Commerce and was also a Director of the London & South Western Railway.

In 1842 the 2nd Earl married Harriet Sophia, daughter of his cousin, Montagu Edmund Parker, and widow of William Coryton. They had two children: Albert Edmund, who became the 3rd Earl, and Emily Katherine. The 2nd Earl's letters to his wife describe a relatively precarious existence blighted by financial worries. In 1842 he wrote that if anyone were to offer him five or six thousand pounds, he would sell a large Van Dyck about to go up to London for an exhibition. But in 1846 Queen Victoria came to Saltram 'and admired the place very much'. Undeterred by his father's experience, the 2nd Earl planned to construct a second costly bridge on the estate the following year. The most renowned engineer of the time, Isambard Kingdom Brunel, submitted a design, but the 2nd Earl was unimpressed: 'I certainly would not meet this fellow again.' In the same year there was anxiety about the servants at Saltram, who were demanding an increase in their wages; a few days later, the Earl explained: 'From no fault of our own, we are very badly off.' Many subsequent letters discuss efforts to persuade Harriet's mother, Mrs Parker of Whiteway, to assist them financially.

To reduce his debts, the 2nd Earl sold off land, including the original home of the Parker family at North Molton. He also tried to increase his long-term income by setting up the Lee Moor Clay

Edmund, 2nd Earl of Morley (1810–64); by Frederick Say (North Stairs 194)

Company in 1852. William Cookworthy had established a china factory in Plymouth in 1768, and by 1815 there were three earthenware potteries in the city. A source of suitable clay had been discovered on the Saltram estate in 1835, which the 2nd Earl hoped to extract profitably by creating a company supported by the Naval Bank. This proved disastrous. The company was poorly managed and failed to produce the expected profits, forcing the 2nd Earl to borrow more and more from the bank. Mrs Parker was finally persuaded to help, and contributed £30,000 towards the business, but without success. In 1861 the bank refused to lend any more money, and the Lee Moor Clay Company crashed.

The 2nd Earl's son described the family's fortunes at this time: 'Saltram was let to Mr. Hartmann ... for £1,000 a year. It was indeed a miserable time and then there seemed to be no hope of recovery. Henceforth we lived abroad, spending part of the year at Whiteway with Mrs Parker and partly in London in houses hired for the season.' In 1864 the 2nd Earl had the second of two strokes probably brought on by his financial anxieties and died. Like his father before him, he left his son debts totalling more than £200,000.

ALBERT EDMUND PARKER, 3RD EARL OF MORLEY
(1843–1905)

Of all the owners of Saltram, the 3rd Earl of Morley is perhaps the most appealing, because he tackled the challenge of saving Saltram, and meticulously recorded his efforts in his letters and journals.

After taking a First at Oxford, the 3rd Earl went into politics as a Liberal, serving as Lord-in-Waiting in Gladstone's first administration. When Gladstone returned to government, he was Under-Secretary for War between 1880 and 1885, the year General Gordon died defending Khartoum. In 1886 the 3rd Earl was appointed a Privy Counsellor and First Commissioner of Works, but soon resigned over Gladstone's decision to grant Home Rule to Ireland. Finally, in 1889 he achieved the prized position of Chairman of Committee, as he announced to his wife: 'This is really grand – I got 95. Balfour got 77 votes.'

*Albert, 3rd Earl of Morley (1843–1905); by Ellis Roberts
(North Stairs)*

In 1876 he had married Margaret Holford, daughter of the immensely wealthy Robert Stayner Holford of Westonbirt, Gloucestershire. Through her, the Parkers later acquired Westonbirt (including the Arboretum), and Dorchester House, the Park Lane mansion designed by Lewis Vulliamy in 1850–63. In keeping with the Saltram tradition of artistic women, Margaret, or 'Minnie', as she was known, was an accomplished artist in watercolour – most of her work is in bound volumes in the Library. The 3rd Earl and his wife had four children: Edmund Robert, Viscount Boringdon, who became the 4th Earl; Montagu Brownlow, who became the 5th Earl; Mary Theresa; and John Holford, whose eldest son became the 6th Earl.

In Devon, the 3rd Earl was much involved with county matters, but most of his energy was spent on removing the burden of financial liabilities inherited from his father and grandfather. In 1897 this burden was further increased when he inherited the Whiteway estate from his mother. However, between 1864 and 1885 he reduced the family debt

from £205,966 to £170,400 (sums which are equivalent to millions of pounds today), and in 1889 wound up the disastrous Lee Moor Clay Company. As a result, the long exile from Saltram came to an end in 1884. The 3rd Earl noted the moment in his diary: 'Fancy my feelings at being with dearest Minnie in our own home after twenty-three years absence – I can hardly believe that I am here again.'

Reinstated at Saltram, the 3rd Earl began a far-reaching programme of repairs and improvements, funded by the sale of the Laira Bridge and carefully chosen paintings by Reynolds and Van Dyck. The house was painted inside and out; the furniture, china and pictures cleaned and restored; electric bells, more central heating and better sewers installed; the kitchen updated and a new staircase built. Elsewhere on the estate, improvements continued. New lodges and farm cottages were constructed, and near the Merafield entrance, the 3rd Earl built a new house for his rotund farm manager, Mr. Vosper: 'Mr. Vosper working on Merafield House, & making a lawn tennis court!! (This may be an economy if it reduces his circumference.)' In 1885 the 3rd Earl calculated that over the previous seventeen years, he had spent the large sum of £16,000 on drainage, building and improvements, and the proposed works were nearly complete, with the exception of three farmhouses and two cottages still to be built. In 1886 he wrote proudly to his wife from Saltram: 'I wish you were here to enjoy the place – it is really looking quite lovely.'

The 3rd Earl and his wife were popular on the estate and in Plymouth society. In 1898 Saltram celebrated the coming-of-age of Viscount Boringdon with a series of parties to include estate staff, tenants, Plymouth society figures and friends of the family, concluding with a garden party for 800 guests. The newspapers described the festivities:

Dinner was served in the Orangery, which had been delightfully decorated under the personal supervision of Earl Morley, and which looked particularly inviting with its banner bedecked walls and its long table which groaned beneath the weight of choice viands and lovely table decorations from the gardens adjoining.

Margaret, Countess of Morley (1855–1908) and her son Edmund; by Ellis Roberts (North Stairs)

EDMUND ROBERT PARKER, 4TH EARL OF MORLEY
(1877–1951)

The 4th Earl inherited Saltram at the age of 28. He was clearly regarded by society as an eligible young man, as one of 'Bob's Letters about Bachelors' in *The Gentlewoman* explained:

My Dear Coz, ... you are ... destined to have one of the best of our English aristocracy as your future husband; so let me tell you this week about a young man I met at a shooting party in Devonshire last year ... His full name is Viscount Boringdon ... He was educated at ... Cambridge, where he made many friends and played a good deal of 'footer' ... I should like to get you his photograph in his magnificent Yeomanry uniform with his slung cape and tight-fitting jacket covered with silver lace ... as he is very tall and has a good figure ... When in Devonshire in the summer months [he] spends most of his time rocking about in a boat with a line, or taking occasional

Boringdon was presented with an illuminated address signed by the estate staff, and the tenants proposed a toast to the Earl, while the band played 'A Fine Old English Gentleman'.

However, not all of the 3rd Earl's tenants regarded him with such warmth. In 1897 he inherited property in Ireland near the Fermanagh/Leitrim border which he sold in 1901 in unfortunate circumstances: since the agricultural depression of the 1880s the tenants had been unable to pay their rents, and the new owners threatened to evict them for non-payment. The sale prompted the following headline: 'Orange & green stand shoulder to shoulder in the fight against landlord injustice. Great meeting on the Morley Estate to protest against the sale over the tenants' heads.'

The 3rd Earl died in 1905. The obituaries referred to him as 'a man of the highest personal character ... His abilities, partly owing to the modesty of his manner, were hardly appreciated by the public ... In Devonshire his name was a household word for courtesy and charity.'

Edmund, 4th Earl of Morley (1877–1951)

During World War II the park was occupied by the American army

trips to and from the Scillies. In appearance he is one of the type we are nationally proudest of, as the product of an English public school and university, and what can I say for him that is better than that?

In fact, the 4th Earl never married, living mostly at Saltram with his brother, Monty, or travelling abroad after the end of the shooting season. Soon after his father's death, he discovered that the cost of running his estates was outstripping their income. Farm rents were still low, following the agricultural depression brought about by imports of cheap American corn, and many landowners had to let or sell their country houses at this time. The 4th Earl let Whiteway in 1911, and used the proceeds to

continue the programme of improvements started by his father, which included building new cottages. In addition, Saltram's first wireless installation was set up at a cost of 10d.

At the end of the First World War, the 4th Earl's sister, Lady Mary, came to live at Saltram with her husband, the Hon. Lionel St Aubyn, son of Lord St Levan of St Michael's Mount. Lady Mary ran the household, and continued to do so until her death in 1932. The last person to be born at Saltram was Lady Mary and Lionel's third son, Thomas. He and his two brothers spent a happy childhood there between the wars, looked after by their nanny. The 4th Earl (known as 'Uncle B') would walk to the Point and back every day, and always read one chapter of his book after lunch, tea and dinner – if one of the boys moved his bookmark back a chapter, he would read the same chapter all over again.

In spite of the 4th Earl's efforts, the cost of maintaining the family estates could not be sustained indefinitely, and difficult decisions had to be made. In 1923 the Whiteway estate was sold, and after inheriting Westonbirt and Dorchester Houses in 1926, the 4th Earl put both up for sale. However, he retained the Arboretum, which was particularly dear to him. He would drive up once a month to oversee the work of the fourteen men employed there – one of their tasks was to make up boxes of flowers to be sent down by train every week to decorate Saltram. According to H. Avray Tipping, writing in *Country Life* in 1926, the 4th Earl 'maintains this fine eighteenth-century house and its priceless contents with exact care and informed judgment'. The fact that Saltram was so well cared for owed much to the eleven house staff, who comprised three housemaids, a housekeeper, butler, first and second footman, odd-job man, kitchenmaid, scullery-maid and cook. Gertrude Antell, who came to Saltram, aged sixteen, as the third housemaid in 1936, was paid 8s a week plus a laundry allowance. Her long working day included making beeswax and turpentine polish for the furniture, and cleaning the carpets with wet newspaper. In 1938 Queen Mary came to tea, and the house staff were given gas fires for their rooms as a special treat.

The Second World War brought great change to Saltram. All but two of the house staff departed, leaving the 4th Earl and his brother to protect Saltram as best they could. Air-raid shelters were dug in the park, and the great Venetian window of the Saloon was bricked up against falling bombs. Plymouth was blitzed early on, Saltram Farm was badly damaged, and a Wellington bomber crashed in a nearby field. The house survived largely thanks to the efforts of the 4th Earl and Monty, both in their sixties, who were regular fire-watchers on the roof. The park was taken over by the American army, which occupied the stable block, and set up a large camp at Merafield Lodge for soldiers assembling for D-Day. Their amphibious craft and equipment were concealed in the woods, and several of the broad concrete roads which they laid in the park are still there. In some respects, however, the old order persisted at Saltram, in spite of the war. The butler and cook stayed on to look after the two elderly gentlemen and the members of the family who visited from time to time.

After the war, Saltram began to return to normal. Work started to repair the damage caused by the incendiary bombs, and nine house staff were appointed. The presence of a near pre-war quota of staff at Saltram was unusual, since the Second World War brought an end to many people's expectation of a career in domestic service in the houses of the wealthy. Electric light was installed for the first time, though only in a limited part of the house. When the bachelor 4th Earl died in 1951, the title passed to his younger brother, Monty.

MONTAGU BROWNLOW PARKER, 5TH EARL OF MORLEY
(1878–1962)

Monty Brownlow Parker became the 5th Earl of Morley at the age of 73. As a young man, he had served as a lieutenant with the Grenadier Guards in the Boer War – some of the remarkable photographs which record his wartime experiences are kept at the Imperial War Museum. In the First World War, he was mentioned in dispatches five times, and received the Croix de Guerre. After the war, when not at Saltram, he would spend his time in London on business trips, or travelling abroad. Between the First and Second World Wars, Thomas St Aubyn and his brothers knew Monty as 'Uncle God'. He was handsome, very well-dressed and enjoyed being in the limelight.

The 5th Earl also had a brief career as an 'archaeologist'. His enthusiasm was fired by the work of Dr Walter Juvelius, a Finnish teacher and poet, who claimed to have discovered coded passages in the Hebrew texts of the Old Testament that revealed the hiding place of the Ark of the Covenant to be beneath the Temple of Jerusalem. The 5th Earl became part of an archaeological expedition to test Dr Juvelius's theory, and in 1909 excavations started below the southern end of the Temple area. 180 labourers were employed to clear centuries of silt and debris from the tunnels, and by 1910 the excavations had reached a point beneath the Mosque of Omar, from where further progress seemed impossible. It was decided to try an approach from above, through the floor of the Mosque itself, and the resident sheikh was therefore bribed with 100 gold sovereigns to allow access to the Mosque after dark. Unfortunately for the excavators, the sheikh's brother got wind of the project, and also demanded payment. When this was refused, he gave the whole show away. Muslim riots ensued, and the 5th Earl and his companions were accused of sacrilege. A newspaper correspondent in Jerusalem reported:

This party of Capt. Parker is probably only an archae-ological association, but rumour willed it otherwise. Every man in the street knows that they have drawn and spent £60,000 during the past two years, and worked the diggers in two sets so as to keep the works going day and night. Their special aim was to possess themselves of the Ark of the Covenant and the crown and sceptre of royal Solomon.

The members of the expedition had to flee for their lives. They had discovered nothing of any significance, but had succeeded in clearing the tunnels ready for the serious archaeological expedi-tions which followed.

At Saltram from 1951, the 5th Earl continued to tackle the damage and backlog of maintenance created by the war years, in the face of serious financial difficulties. The London firm Keeble's redecorated the principal rooms, and new blue silk damask was woven in Lyon for the Saloon walls and Chippendale furniture, at a cost of £25,000. Outside, the south and west fronts were re-rendered, and the roofs repaired. To help pay the mounting costs of maintenance, Saltram's great kitchen garden was let.

The 4th Earl's death in 1951 had imposed a heavy burden of death-duties on the estate, and by 1953 Saltram's finances were so precarious that serious action was required to save it from ruin. Lady Astor, the MP for Plymouth between 1919 and 1945, suggested that the best way to preserve Saltram for the future might be to give it to the National Trust. Negotiations therefore began to reclaim the death-duties which had already been paid, handing over, instead, the house with its prin-cipal contents and 291 acres of parkland. The trans-action was financed by the National Land Fund, set up in memory of those who died in the Second World War, and completed in 1957. The National Trust acquired Saltram, and the 5th Earl retained a lease of the whole house for his lifetime.

A key figure in the acquisition of Saltram by the National Trust was Michael Trinick, the Trust's representative in the West Country. Once the nego-tiations were complete, he commented: 'Despite the efforts of the 5th Earl the house was by now in disas-trously bad repair. The roofs leaked throughout the house, there were three major outbreaks of dry rot, no external painting had been done for many years.' The restoration of Saltram began, directed by the first Curator, Nigel Neatby, and carried out by the estate staff, notably members of the Bowman family.

Like his brother, the 5th Earl never married, and on his death in 1962, the title passed to his nephew, Lt Col. John St Aubyn Parker, who had seen action in North-West Europe and Korea. He was Lord Lieutenant of Devon in 1982–98.

In accordance with the 5th Earl's wishes, the Trust took on full responsibility for Saltram's upkeep, assisted by income from visitors and the sale of part of the contents. Saltram is also depen-dent on annual grants from English Heritage. Research continues to restore the historic appear-ance of the house and its grounds.

America: detail of the inlaid top of the Boulle table in the Staircase Hall

John Parker and his sister Theresa as children; by Joshua Reynolds, 1779

THE GARDEN, PARK AND ESTATE

THE GARDEN

The garden is situated on a ridge, which falls away steeply to the north, towards the Laira (as the Plym estuary is known), and more gently to the south, with a vista of parkland turning gradually into farmland. Little is known about its appearance in the first half of the eighteenth century, but the main garden walks, Amphitheatre and Fanny's Bower were probably all introduced by John and Lady Catherine Parker after 1743, together with the statues by Cheere on the west front. Charles Hamilton, the creator of the great landscape garden at Painshill, may also have advised the Parkers. Lady Catherine's brother wrote to her from his house at Hinton St George, Somerset:

Mr. Hamilton, a son of Lord Abercones, who has that pretty place so near London, and who (now Mr. Kent is dead) is certainly the top man of taste in England, has been here for some days, to whom I am very much obliged for the visit as well as the advice and assistance he has been so good as to give me here ... I therefore in return have promised to shew him Mr. Balls, yr. Ladyships (who may also profit of it) and Lord Edgecombes.

Theresa Parker had grand plans for both the inside and outside of Saltram. In 1771 she was thinking of building a summer-house and wanted to enlist her elder brother's help: 'Pray do not forget the castle. I know I ought to apply to Fritz to remind you of it from time to time, something must be built upon that spot and I know no other plan will ever please me so much as yours did, as far as I saw it.' The Castle is the octagonal building with battlements, situated at the western end of the garden. It was built in the early 1770s, probably by the estate carpenter, Mr Stockman, over an existing sixteenth- or seventeenth-century structure. It would have been used as an eating-room, but primarily as a place where visitors could pause on garden walks and enjoy the views out to the park.

From the early 1770s, the Saltram account books regularly record the name of Nathaniel Richmond, garden designer, who was probably introduced to the Parkers by their friends, the Pelhams of Stanmer Park, Brighton. Humphry Repton wrote of Richmond:

He understood perfectly how to give the most natural shape to artificial ground, how to dress walks in a pleasure garden, and how to leave or plant picturesque groups of trees, his lines were generally graceful and easy, but his knowledge of the Art was rather Technical and executive, than theoretical; he could stake out the detached parts of a place with much taste, but of the great outline he had so little idea that he never delivered any general plan.

Richmond appears to have been involved in laying out the garden and park. He also submitted designs for garden buildings, including the Orangery, which was erected in 1773, after modifications by Stockman, on the site of an earlier building. The design may have been based on Adam's similar proposal for an orangery at Croome Court in Worcestershire. In 1774 Theresa was considering how to decorate the interior. She wanted 'Niches and Statues for the Summer, exposed as it is, to the Sea air, and the Dampness there must be in the Walls sets aside all thoughts of Paintings ... I have a notion we may get good Medallions and Bas Reliefs in Artificial Stone, which properly arranged over Niches may make it clever'. In 1782 an orange grove was created behind the Chapel as a summer location for the trees which over-wintered in the Orangery.

In the spring of 1777 a party of women came to Saltram and found a garden filled with the most popular formal features of the time:

We viewed the chapple that's building, the Banquetting House then filled with greens, near it a large Eagle. We walked through the plantation by the Cold Bath, through the Wood to the Temple of Jupiter which is [in] a ruinous state, however as it rained were glad to partake of our cold meat. Then we set out walking again. Saw a very natural cave made of petrifactions & stellatates, a Grotto with shells, then back to the house till the chaises we[re] ready.

Work on the Chapel had begun in 1776. Converted from an old shippon (cow byre), it may have been created as a memorial to Theresa, who had died in 1775. Stockman added battlements and buttresses, installed large pointed windows and applied render to the walls. It is now an art gallery. The 'Cold Bath' was situated at the Point, and cropped up regularly in family correspondence, since sea-bathing was considered beneficial on health grounds. The Temple of Jupiter may have been the original name for Fanny's Bower, the small garden temple situated in Saltram Wood behind the Orangery, which was given its present name by the National Trust in memory of Fanny Burney's visit with a royal party in 1789. The 'Grotto with shells' may be a reference to the Amphitheatre below Saltram Wood on the banks of the Laira, which has grotto-like arches on either side of the main structure. It would originally have provided excellent views out across the river for guests taking a walk through the grounds, and would have impressed visitors arriving by boat, as depicted in William Tomkins's painting of 1770 (no. 166; Garden Room).

In 1771 the kitchen garden was moved to a new location near the Merafield entrance, allowing the park to flow around the house in the eighteenth-century manner. In 1772 Anne Robinson reported to her elder brother: 'The new garden is a very fine one and will be very usefull in two years time but at present there is nothing to be had in it but Melons.' Hot-houses were added later, which produced grapes, peaches, nectarines and figs. By 1900, the kitchen garden comprised six acres, with about a mile of wall, and six new glasshouses. It was not acquired by the Trust with the rest of the park, and was largely demolished in the 1980s to make way for a small housing estate.

In 1785 Lord Boringdon reported: 'I have just finished my Plantation on top of the Hill, wch. already begins to look beautifull. It has however been a very heavy & expensive jobb. The Peach House will be quite compleated by the middle of next week, when my works will all be at an end.' On his death, Anne Robinson took charge of the park and garden until her nephew came of age. In 1788 she wrote to her sister-in-law: 'The Orange Trees are all put into the Green House and I shall begin planting next week. Tomorrow I begin to cut down the Scotch Firs which will give me great satisfaction. I was two hours with the Gardener marking those that were to come down, it is many

The Orangery, which was built in 1773

The Amphitheatre at Saltram in 1771; by William Tomkins (no. 168; Garden Room)

more than I thought, and still I have spared many that should come down.'

The 1st Earl of Morley was too preoccupied with expensive engineering projects on the estate to devote much time to the garden. In 1822 Saltram was described as standing 'on a lawn of 300 acres, surrounded by extensive plantations'. Engravings from the same period also show that the garden still retained the eighteenth-century layout of grassed areas and trees, with few flowers.

The 3rd Earl started to bring the garden up to date in 1877, consulting the Veitches of Exeter, one of the most important dynasties of Victorian nurserymen. Rare and tender plants and unusual trees were also purchased from Jeffreys of Ciren-cester. Many plants came from his mother's garden at Whiteway, and others were gifts from keen gardeners, including A. G. Mitford of Batsford, and the 3rd Earl's father-in-law, R. S. Holford, from his

famous arboretum at Westonbirt. The 3rd Earl laid out a parterre next to the west front of the house, with small circular and rectangular flower-beds interspersed with urns, arranged around a circular pond. Off the east front, there was a parterre of about six star-shaped flower-beds, and a further, daisy-shaped parterre in front of the Orangery. A new fountain and rockery were installed in the orange grove, and an escallonia hedge planted at the south-west corner of the house, to separate the garden from the gravelled area in front. The lime avenue may also date from the late nineteenth century. In 1891 400 trees in the park and garden were blown down in a gale.

Since 1900, the formal flower-beds have all been grassed over, restoring the eighteenth- and early nineteenth-century appearance of these areas. Otherwise, the 4th and 5th Earls seem to have been content to preserve the garden created by previous generations, rather than make major changes, and the National Trust adopted a similar approach when it acquired Saltram in 1957. Early work concentrated on improving the lawns and thickening the boundary of shrubs and trees, to act as a shelterbelt and screen the unsightly cement works and rubbish tip from view. In 1963 a ha-ha was dug in front of the house, and the escallonia hedge removed, so that the garden would be protected from the livestock in the surrounding fields by a less obtrusive barrier.

THE WEST FRONT

The west front is perhaps the most successful of the three mid-eighteenth-century façades. It is composed of a central block linked by low wings to pavilions, but, as with the east front, symmetry has been achieved only with the use of false windows. The coupling of therm and Venetian windows in the wings, and the niches in the pavilions, distract the eye from the lack of horizontal alignment in the windows and roofs, but from the west lawn the earlier building can clearly be seen breaking the roofline of the Parkers' house. The false door in the middle of the façade reflects the mid-eighteenth-century appearance of the entrance on the south front.

SCULPTURE

The statues in the niches are by perhaps John Cheere (1709–87) and represent, from left to right: *Mercury*, *Isis*, *A Vestal Virgin* and *Antinous*. The sphinxes are also by Cheere, and flanked the main entrance to the house until the 1st Earl added the porch, when they were moved to the Orangery.

THE PARK AND ESTATE

Donne's map of 1765 shows Saltram's spectacular location, on a natural peninsula between the Laira and Chelson Creek. The main access at that date was via a tidal crossing over the Laira, from Crabtree to Blaxton Point. Surrounded by ancient

Distant view of Saltram, 1778: by William Tomkins (no. 163; Garden Room)

woodland to the north, Saltram had excellent views south and west across the estuary to Plymouth and Mount Edgcumbe, which can now mostly be appreciated only from the pictures in the Garden Room.

The Parkers were keen agricultural improvers. In 1773 Theresa wrote to her brother: 'The whole Down that you may remember between Boringdon and Cann Quarry, besides two Hundred acres of the same sort of Furze Brake, is now covered with all sorts of Corn and affords a prospect of Plenty that is really very striking.' The Parkers considered agricultural land to be visually pleasing, and so the park boundaries have always been lightly defined, particularly to the south, where the parkland merges into park-like farmland. By this time, at least, there were deer in the park, although they had disappeared by the 1860s.

Lord Boringdon created a more impressive approach to the park by building the Longbridge Drive about 1770 on an embankment across Plympton marshes, north of the house; soon after, the enclosed marshland was turned into a meadow. In 1771 Theresa wrote that they were thinking of 'building one of the Stanmer Lodges at the entrance of the new road by the Embankment'. The new lodge seems to have been based on the lower lodges at Stanmer Park, and probably survived until the 3rd Earl's time.

In 1772 Robert Adam designed Stag Lodges for a site close to the present main entrance to the park, Merafield. The statues of the stags, chosen by the Parkers in preference to Adam's lions, were not added to the flanking piers until 1783. The connecting arch originally intended by Adam was probably never built. Stag Lodges were moved to their present location at the eastern entrance to the park by the 1st Earl, and replaced with a new lodge in 1900 by the 3rd Earl at Merafield.

The stable block was begun in the 1740s by John and Lady Catherine Parker. The earliest section, the pedimented north range, seems to relate to the stable wings shown in the drawing illustrated on p.44. The coach-house range was added in the 1760s, as were the cupola and turret clock over the north range. The clock movement of 1761 is by William Smith of Upper Moorfields, and the bell is dated 1765. Lord Boringdon was particularly keen on horse-racing, and made frequent trips to Newmarket and Epsom, where his horse 'Saltram' won the Derby in 1783. He also established a much-admired racing stud at Saltram, and when he decided to sell his horses in 1784, several were purchased by the Prince of Wales. The 1st Earl built the present south range of the stable block early in the nineteenth century, and although he owned no racehorses, created a race-course on reclaimed land at Chelson Meadow.

Projects outside the park seem to have occupied much of the 1st Earl's time. A short-lived iron-ore mine at the south of the estate was opened in 1839, while a great limekiln owned by the family at Crabtree was used to convert the local limestone into fertilizer for farmland. Inside the park, the 1st Earl continued to plant trees and remove hedges. To the south-west of the garden he established a new area of woodland called The Belt, so that the park was almost entirely bounded by trees, in the manner of 'Capability' Brown. He also created his own new eastern approach to the house, via Hardwick Wood. At this point, the Saltram estate comprised more than 4,000 acres, including Boringdon to the north, Plympton to the east, and the south bank of the Laira as far as Laira Bridge (see p. 52).

The 2nd Earl set up the Lee Moor Clay Company to promote mining on a site north-east of Saltram, and extended the railway, which cut across the northern end of the park, near Marsh Mills. The 3rd Earl planted many new trees in the park, including box elder, water fir, elm and sycamore, and herbaceous perennials, such as gunnera and miscanthus.

In 1957 the National Trust acquired 291 acres of the park, and has since bought additional parts of the estate. In the early 1960s Chelson Meadow was purchased by Plymouth City Council and became the council tip. The outskirts of Plymouth have expanded up to the edges of the park, and in 1970 it was cut in two by the new Plympton bypass, the A38. Today Saltram is virtually surrounded by modern development.